W9-BFB-226

*"Dandelion, Dandelion, with my breath
I set you free to travel the four corners of the
world where hope creates change and change
makes dreams come true."*

*Barbara*

Wishes for a Mother's Heart™

Copyright © 2010 by Wishes, Inc

All rights reserved. No part of this book may be reproduced or transmitted in any form or by any means without written permission from the author.

Book Design: www.doghaus.net
Edits: Julia Altott
Editor: Lyndsay Malloy Cherry, Muna Deriane and Barbara Kay Collins
ISBN **978-0-615-34429-4**

We hope you enjoy this book published by Wishes, Inc.
For more information on the Wish project and product please visit
www.wishesfortheheart.com

Printed in USA by 48HrBooks (www.48HrBooks.com)

*To our mothers:*
*Jean, Patricia, and Ellie*

# CONTENTS

## WISHES FOR THE HEART

## WISHES TO SHARE

## ABOUT

# Introductions

# Forward by Leeza Gibbons

There is nothing like a mother's love. In all the world, it is unique. It endures, sustains, supports, and heals even without being asked to do so. It is the most reliable and sturdy force most of us will ever experience. Our mothers are our compasses, our sails, and anchors throughout life; guiding us, challenging us, and encouraging us as we come to the ultimate realization that we are separate from the one who gave us life. Even though we know we came through our moms to be our own people, and as mothers we let go of our children to let them find their own identities, we are connected forever in a way that feels more permanent than our time here on earth.

Maternal energy is everywhere. Being biologically bound does not make a mother…being heart connected does. This book is about all those who have given birth and all those who mother without ever being pregnant. It is about the strongest desires of a mother's heart and the most vulnerable corners of her soul.

This book is written by mothers for mothers. The words come in the form of Wishes, which are gifts we offer to ourselves and others. They are always available, they always fit, and they can be made public or kept secret. A Wish is offered with the purest intention and then released. A Wish shared between women is, in my opinion, a very sacred thing.

My good friend, Tricia LaVoice, began putting thoughts, feelings, and emotions in her written Wishes as a way of healing the hearts of her fellow mothers who were hurting or in pain. That's how I connected with Tricia at the play-yard where our young children went to school. She had been reaching out to her friend Barbara Lazaroff, another mom from school, through "Wishes" designed to support Barbara through a difficult time. I knew immediately this was a special gift and should be shared. Then, my heart was broken after my marriage ended, and Tricia's soft and gentle words given to me in a Wish gave me the courage to face each new challenge.

This triangle of shared love and support was never meant to stay between us. Tricia always saw it as a circle, a sisterhood- and my part was to help open the blanket and wrap it around as many hearts as possible. I read the first Wish Tricia wrote for me, I Wish for You, The Love of Friendship, on the air during my syndicated radio show, Hollywood Confidential. We have about 100 stations in the United States and Canada, and I think all three and a half million of our listeners responded to those powerful words! "An exposed heart appreciates that which is oblivious to the secured" she wrote, and she said, "be free to be weak." It was the beginning of my journey to recover my soul and reclaim my life.

Tricia's words elicited a huge response from my listeners, as I know they will with you. Her special and beautiful friendship with Barbara is so moving and so touching that theirs is a pairing that is stronger because of the very nature of the union.

Let Tricia's words speak to you or someone you love and then allow Barbara to help you put the Wish into action in your own life. These two friends combine their love and their talents to offer you "Wishes for a Mother's Heart." If you keep this book for yourself, I hope you find it to be a blessing in your life as it has been in mine. If you are giving it to someone you love, I hope the words will float like the seeds of a dandelion, landing softly where they need to be.

*Love and More,*
Leeza Gibbons

# What is a Wish?
## Barbara Lazaroff

Wishes are our hearts' desire. As children we daydream, imagining what we will become, what we will look like, who we will marry, what our children will be like, and what adventures we will have. When we are quite young, we often believe we can create that perfect fantasy world by merely conjuring it up and asking for it with magical words or prayer. Sometimes we think that what we covet will find us wherever we are because we are lucky or special.

As we become more mature, most of us learn that "the harder we try, the more luck we seem to have." Instead of seeking and striving with sustained hard work or education, some people feel entitled. Others become stagnant due to insecurity or failure and find it difficult to attempt reaching for their goals, afraid to stumble yet again.

Wishes are wonderful moments of fancy, and dreaming is an essential human process that has allowed for miraculous scientific discoveries, breathtaking fine art, and other masterful works of humankind. However, these realized dreams were always partnered with study or practice, knowledge and talent, all requiring enormous effort of mind, spirit and body. To see our hopes and desires realized, we must put genuine concerted effort into taking the steps to create the life we wish to live. Not unlike learning to walk or talk, raising a child, tending a garden, learning to play an instrument, becoming a graceful dancer or a talented athlete, there is a great deal of thought, planning, practice and failure before there is success.

One of my treasured quotes reminds us that, "Courage doesn't always roar. Sometimes courage is the quiet voice at the end of the day saying, 'I will try again tomorrow." The Wishes in this book are meant to inspire, illuminate, touch and motivate the reader to think deeply, as well as to move you viscerally. They are words that will resonate with both the mind and the body. Each reader will be attracted to and affected by certain words or phrases, or themes; often this is very telling, highly personal. Are you particularly moved by the Wish concerning security, comfort, loss, forgiveness, anger, or personal change? Often the Wishes will clarify and highlight for you what you are most enveloped in at that moment in your life. Always, the Wishes will reveal to you that we all share similar joys, fears, concerns and aspirations. As you change, your attraction to certain Wishes may alter as well, but they each possess universal emotions that speak to various times in our lives that most of us can profoundly relate to, echoing our most authentic self.

My welcome challenge is to respond emotionally to Tricia's beautiful, poetic words, and attempt to guide the reader in a pragmatic direction. By asking the reader to embrace these words and insights in their hearts and then transmit them to "hands" moving forward into actions. I hope to provide some constructive advice on how to own a Wish with purpose and passion and create your own personal identity and forge your own reality. Dreams are the inspiration of action, but only by taking action towards your goals can you provide real change and fulfillment in your life.

I will provide practical, creative and dynamic solutions, opportunities and projects to move the Wishes into the realm of substance. I want to explore some of the steps you can pursue to perhaps change your job, realize your potential, enhance friendships and family relationship, by learning to be a kinder, more compassionate and communicative individual. Be a chameleon and recreate yourself; exercise how to progress, as we must all do, as life itself progresses. I would like to encourage you to assemble an emotional arsenal so that you can approach every day with the attitude that "this is an exciting challenge that I will overcome with my unique skills," rather than relying on old patterns of fear of failure, believing a difficult situation is always an insurmountable obstacle.

Wishes may sound ambitious; none of us are licensed therapists, nor are our lives "perfect," whatever that would look like. Our strength and wisdom comes from our experiences and camaraderie. Thank you Leeza for your profoundly touching foreward illuminating the guiding power of maternal love. We are loving and trusting friends and mothers; we have all experienced marriage, and two have endured divorce. We have experienced losses, loves, betrayals, disappointments, triumphs, failures and enormous change as many women have. Tricia and I are going to share of ourselves and give the best we can to enhance, inspire and hopefully positively affect people to expand their lives. Some readers may need to change direction, others require techniques or inspiration to "hang in there," others to move past the past, and all of us need to remember never to forget to laugh.

As resourceful, positive-thinking women; we have seen what can be accomplished with vision followed by hard work, creative solutions, redirection, personal introspection, the power of partnering, mentoring, friendship, community, love and the will of the individual.

I will try with genuine concern to Wish and imagine along with Tricia, analyze and explore. I will work earnestly to engineer some of the valuable patterns and strategies one might employ to wishimagineer a dream come true.

*If you can dream it, you can do it!*
Barbara

# How the Wishes First Began
## Tricia LaVoice

When I think of the *Wishes* and how they started, I do not know where to begin, so I will bring you back to the summer of 2005. I had just finished writing my first novel, *Pieces of My Mother*, my journey of accepting the sudden death of my mother and father twelve years earlier from an automobile accident. After the death of my parents, two very special women came into my life, offering me the unconditional love and support I needed to restore my faith and trust in life, allowing me to be the mother and wife I wished to be for my family. I questioned if my mother had sent them to me. Barbara Lazaroff was one of those women who became family to me.

As all of us do, Barbara had her share of hardships. September of 2005 brought with it some new challenges and Barbara was not anticipating the month to be a good one. She had been such a loving and supportive friend as I wrote my manuscript, on top of making my four children feel special. It was my turn to give back to her. As we sat on her back patio that late August afternoon, I pledged to be a non-complaining friend void of all issues and problems the whole month of September. "In fact," I suggested, "I will not only be the best listener in the world, I will '*wish*' you something every night."

So that is how it started, good listening skills followed by a simple email saying, "good morning" or "good night," depending on how promptly I could get to my computer, with a simple *Wish:* "Today, September 1st, 2005, I wish for you, Trust" or "Compassion," etc. However, shortly into the month, life reminded us of how fragile and unforeseen it can be. September 6th, Hurricane Katrina hit the American coast, causing unfathomable damage. September 8th, my husband's job confirmed that my family would need to relocate to the Hartford area of Connecticut. And, the early morning of September 11th, I was woken by the phone to the sounds of my sister's voice telling me to come home; her son, my nephew, Aaron, had tragically died at the age of nineteen. Again, Barbara became support for me and my family. I continued writing *Wishes* as an outlet during the week I spent with my sister and her family. Upon returning to Los Angeles, September continued on its path of uncertainties. Barbara experienced some unexpected medical troubles along with personal issues to accompany the anticipated problems she faced. Over the month, the *Wishes* became personal and profound, documenting the events that unfolded.

At the time, Leeza's children attended the same school as Barbara's and mine. I spoke with her only occasionally, but I was always comforted by her true kindness and sincerity. How it came about that I spoke to her on the recess yard and frantically divulged the month's heartbreaks, I do not know. In my frenzy, I also told her about writing Barbara *Wishes*, and how I was documenting the month in a way I could never have imagined in August. That night, Leeza sent me an email, a *Wish* for peace in my life. This was the start of our friendship. Over the next months, I found a treasured trust and loyalty in Leeza, a sisterhood, as if we had been friends all our lives.

I stayed in Los Angeles and finished out the school year with the children as my husband dutifully commuted back and forth from the East Coast. Leaving California and the comfort of all my friends was, to say the least, very difficult for me. My nephew's death and the painful memories it dug up made me that much more dependent on my friends Barbara and Leeza for support. I left Los Angeles that summer brokenhearted. September 2006, I wrote *Wishes* once more, but they lacked luster as I struggled to adjust and acclimate four children into a new lifestyle.

Over my first year in Connecticut, I was met with one of the toughest times of my life. Simply, I was miserable. My husband was working hard at a new position and away from the home a lot. The children were off at school and trying to make new friends. I spent much of my time alone, something I had never done before in my life. Although I still spoke to Barbara and Leeza and other friends, it was hard to maintain the same level of friendship without the day-to-day involvement. My life experiences had left me with the fear of loss and I struggled to hold onto my friendships, people I considered family, but that is hard to do with 3,000 miles between you. I cannot tell you if, had I not lost so many family members unexpectedly, my friends would have mattered so much to me. Life challenges all of us in one way or another and most people need friends to help them through. I certainly did.

It was the first time since my parents' death, and Aaron's death, that I was alone with my thoughts. I had no choice but to confront the pain in front of me and walk right through it. I had never felt so alone, but I am a survivor and yearned for peace and happiness in my life. I began taking peaceful walks and sorting through all my thoughts. As the summer reached an end, I was unsure if I would write *Wishes*, but come September 1st, I sent one off to Barbara. By September 6th, she had recognized that my time alone had offered me insight and she suggested I share the *Wishes* with others. Later in the month, I met Leeza in Manhattan while she was there working on a Sheer Coverage photo shoot. I mentioned to her that I was writing *Wishes* again. Leeza loved the concept and encouraged me to write beyond September. As time went on, I began writing *Wishes* for all the people in my life. Then, in late October, while searching through a box that had gotten misplaced in the shuffle, I found a light blue leather pouch that Leeza had given me two years earlier, containing a pretty pair of earrings and embroidered across the pouch read the word *WISH*. It was then that we knew it was time to print these *Wishes*.

These *Wishes* are my thoughts that stem from all the love in my life from my husband, children, sisters, friends, and from all the love my parents gave me while they were with me. These *Wishes* also stem from all the pain I have endured in my life that has opened my heart to great depth to appreciate that love. They belong to all and confirm that the greatest gift, the most powerful force the universe has to offer us, is that of human kindness.

*Love,*
*Tricia*

Wishes and Reflections written by Tricia LaVoice
Words and Actions shared by Barbara Lazaroff

# Wishes for the Heart

We gave careful consideration to dividing this chapter up into two sections: Wishes for the mother's heart and Wishes for the child's heart; however, we elected to leave it as one. In every mother's heart lies a child in need of love and support. Every mother is someone's daughter and she is deserving of maternal love all of her life.

# For you, I Wish
## The Beauty of a Dandelion

*"Let her be," I heard the older child whisper to the younger. "Please!" "No, she's resting." I lie half awake, nursing a headache as my children congregated outside my door. Time passed and again I heard their voices. "Now?" "No." Curiosity over my child's impatience and excitement prevailed, so I called out for him to come. He ran to my bed side yelling, "Mommy, Mommy! Look, I picked you a beautiful flower!" The proud twinkle in his eyes accompanied his smile that started in his heart and traveled through his tender seven–year-old body before exploding onto his face. He reached out his hand, opening his tightly gripped fingers, and laid a freshly picked dandelion beside me. The dandelion, labeled a weed in the book of science, is discarded from our gardens and rarely set on our tables. I picked up the white fluffy gift beside me and searched for a scent I knew was not there. I thought of you, knowing that you are feeling discarded, unappreciated at this juncture of your life. My vision holds a different view. I remember your laughter like a field of daises and I see your smile in a bundle of sunflowers. I look to you and see the grace of a lily, the complexity of an orchid, and the sweetness of a lilac. But my image of you holds little importance without your embrace. Take a moment and picture the world without flowers. I look to her for lessons knowing that beauty lies deeper than the eye can see. Unlike the rock, strong and independent, she is fragile and vulnerable. She allows herself to need the grace of others for her survival, calling on the soil for nourishment, the rain to quench her thirst, and the sun to warm her petals. In gratitude she gives back and changes the world with her fragrance and beauty. She is a treasure, a healer, as is human kindness. Let the words of those who love you be your soil and nourish your soul, let their compassion be your rain and quench your thirst for love, let their laughter be your sun and warm your heart. Allow yourself to need and be needed. For you, I wish the beauty of a dandelion.*

"My vision holds a different view"

– Tricia LaVoice

# Reflection

*There are many windows in our home, and you will have a different view of our yard depending on which one you are looking out of. My bedroom window overlooks a big tree which is bare all winter long, blossoms in spring, and then remains beautifully green the rest of the year. My youngest son requested to leave the spray painted snow from the holidays on his windows all year long, and then the windows in the family room are always a bit dusty, either from my poor housekeeping skills or a wind that must continuously blow dust on that side of the house. Depending on which window you are looking out of, you will have a different view of our backyard, regardless of the fact that the yard itself remains constant. Life is a bit like this too. Our perception of our world, regardless of what is reality, is what influences our thoughts the most. Of course, circumstance comes into play and it is much easier to have positive thoughts when life is being kinder to you. My one dear friend Sheila and I talk every Monday morning to catch up after the weekend. She lives by the beach in Los Angeles and I live in the woods in Connecticut. During the winter months, many Mondays are freezing and gray in Connecticut and I will be feeling disheartened, while Sheila will sound chipper as she walks her dog along the pier in 70-degree weather. Sometimes she has to remind me that once the sun shines and the flowers blossom, things will look different.*

*It is important to recognize the outside forces that are affecting your thoughts, and separate them from how you are truly feeling. Perception, just like the weather, can change, but unlike the weather, our perception is in our control. Change your thoughts and the whole world changes. It is much easier to change our thoughts than we may think. Like any bad habit, negative thinking can be corrected when exercised. Leeza is so very generous with her compliments to me, and periodically she will mail me words of encouragement, telling me what a wonderful person she thinks I am. I pin them up on my vision board and know my family will read them, thinking Leeza has no idea that I am not nearly as sweet as she believes. My behavior may come off sweet, but my thoughts can be negative before I massage them to be kinder. It is important for me to see my world lovingly and peacefully. When I catch myself thinking negatively about something, I try to pull my thoughts over to the positive. The more I practice positive thinking, the easier it is to envision my world as a kinder and gentler place and, as a result, the kinder and gentler my world becomes.*

*Having a positive perception is never more vital than when perceiving yourself. But who are you? Are you who YOU think you are or are you how other people perceive you to be? Everyone in the world can think we are wonderful but if we do not believe that none of that matters; it is our perception of ourselves that matters.*

*As mothers, having a healthy perception of ourselves is imperative since children are sensitive to their mother's sense of self-worth. Children will gain their own self-worth and strength from a mother who likes herself and, most important, respects herself. But it is easy to think negatively of oneself and, for that reason, takes less effort. On the other hand, it takes courage, confidence, and action to think positively, and we must always remember that our children are watching how we act and will emulate what they observe.*

*Writing this book makes my heart grow, but having the courage to get it to you is a challenge for me. I have a message from Barbara, whose note sits next to Leeza's note on my vision board, that reads, "I Wish you the realization that perseverance does spawn victory and success. I Wish you the realization that you are your own mirror, that what you project, you must first believe for others to believe it as well." I read those words when I need a little encouragement, but I gain most of my courage to believe in myself when one of my children says something encouraging about my writing. When I see them believing in me, I know I cannot let them down. I believe so they can believe.*

"Our perception of our world, regardless of what is reality,

is what influences us the most."

- Tricia LaVoice

Read Hans Christian Anderson's The Proud Little Apple Blossom. It is about the dandelion's true beauty, misunderstood by the apple blossom. Read it to your child, and then allow your "inner child" to absorb the loveliness and profound lesson.

- Read 17-year-old poet Perre Shelton's poem Dandelion, about his mother's extraordinary, transcendent dignity.
- She was not a rose; she was far more majestic. Poor in earthly possessionsbut wealthy in spirit; and beloved by her son. (Perre Shelton's reading of his poem Dandelion from Def Jam Poetry is available for viewing on YouTube.)

# *Words and Actions from Barbara*

The dandelion is actually many delicate tiny flowers gathered together. Each of these tiny flowers produces a seed attached to a stem with white fluffy threads; one portion is actually called a "wishie!" As a child they delighted me; with my breath I had the power within me to send these fluffy messengers of my fanciful notions off to places unknown. As I watched them gracefully fluttering away, I was joyful and anticipatory. I was certain once the dandelion was fittingly remembered with beloved childhood feelings, (rather than as the adult gardener's commonplace lawn nuisance); it could resume its rightful honor as a magical wand of childlike empowerment! As with so many things in life, the dandelion's image and worth was all a matter of perspective.

- *Start by deciding you are uniquely able, and affirm that you are a valuable person. (List your assets, your skills, talents, what you appreciate about yourself; ask others what they find distinctive about you.)*

- *We need to confirm that we are who we know ourselves to be, not how others alone see us. (Our self worth should be determined by character and spirit, not by what car we drive or what purse we carry. People sometimes make poor character and worth assessments about others in this celebrity driven, monetary society; your value should not be determined by how others with shallow ideals treat you. If you are kind, respectful, honest, hard working, a good citizen and concerned family member, you are indeed a person of enormous substance!)*

- *If you want the world to truly see you, you must open that window to yourself for others to view in.*

- *You do not need a complete makeover to feel renewed. Start with the simplest yet most important of elements: smile. People will smile back.*

- *Say "hello"; people will respond and you will feel immediately more connected to the world around you.*

- *Practice self reflection; what do you like about yourself? Learn to meditate, think deeply find a place you can be silent. (These are examples of an internal process.) What would you like to change or improve? (Perhaps keep a journal of your likes and dislikes, and a plan for self improvement: school, exercise, mindful eating, (healthier cuisine), this is an action project, both short and long term).*

- *Create a personal self-affirming mantra, (something as simple as: "I am wonderful and valuable," or "I can do it" or "today I will..." and decide what you will work towards for that day.)*

- *You must be ready for the change or it will not be effective. You must decide you want to change and are ready to meet the consequences of your transformation; it will be hard work. You will discover the greater the change, the more time and effort you must exert. Perhaps years of study, vigorous exercise, or an unpaid internship, some of the process may be frustrating at first, but you need to commit to persevering.*

These lines are extracted from Nelson Mandela's 1994 inaugural speech; they were actually composed by poet Marianne Williamson. This is one of my favorite mantras. Look it up and read it in its full glory:

"Our deepest fear is not that we are inadequate. Our deepest fear is that we are powerful beyond measure. It is our light, not our darkness that frightens us." "It's not just in some of us; it is in every one. And as we light our own, we unconsciously give other people permission to do the same."

## Beauty in Your Distinctive Way

*Enchantment, the exuberant diversity in a field of wildflowers;*
   *Aromatic harmony, staccato essences.*
   *Silken, velvet, prickly, translucent tissue fine; youthful moist*
   *sensual pizzicato textures trill as they are plucked and pulled.*
*The poised chorus line, not in line, but dotted across the verdant stage,*
   *Captured in place, at repose, beautiful but not free*
   *Liberated by hand to a jar to linger,*
   *Admired, adored, but gone too soon, too fragile to remain.*
   *Stronger in the earth.*
*The quiet dandelion whispers, "Come to me, come closer,*
   *With your life-breath scatter me to the wind so I might travel*
   *See the world; share my magic with all the flowers of the field."*
   *Modest dandelions; graceful dancers, arabesque, plié, relevé,*
   *as they float away*
*Skybound they glance below, the wildflowers lean and sway,*
   *some standing tall, others bending to the winds, some begin to bow.*
*Dandelion, you have found beauty in your distinctive way.*

- Barbara Lazaroff

# For You, I Wish
## Trust

*I love you, yes, you know this. However, I search my heart deep to like you in this moment. I call on myself for compassion and patience to understand you, yet I am challenged by my wounded heart. In your time of turmoil you shut your doors, build windowless walls, and retreat to your cave. I must respect your choice, but you have stayed away too long and loved ones hurt in your departure of them. Adversity spares no one and we are all deserving our healings and dealings. However, we are social creatures, webs of emotion touching one another with our joys and sorrows, and must remain accountable to one another. The line between self-evolvement and responsibility is fine. We search books and worship, turn to dependencies for relief, neglecting to look for clarity in the one place it may rest most. To emerge from your place of pain, to find answers to your questions, you must start from within. You do not dare look within, for you fear of what you will see; I understand, it is scary. Our hardships are our greatest teachers, but our vision is blurred if we do not look to understand the pupil. I remain loyal to you, holding up the bridge that connects you to me, but I fear my arms are weakening. I will not abandon you, for unconditional love will not allow it. Put down your walls, emerge from your cave, and trust human kindness to be waiting for you. For you, I wish trust.*

"I will not abandon you,

for unconditional love

will not allow it."

– Tricia LaVoice

# Reflection

*This Wish was actually written for a very good friend of mine who was going through a difficult time in her life. We chose to include it in the mother's collection due to the response we received from Leeza's listeners. Mothers of both male and female teenagers wrote that they gave the Wish to their teenagers in hopes to open some form of communication with their children.*

*Every time my heart starts to pound and my stomach flip-flops with worry that there is something wrong with my teenagers, I ask myself: Why do they get so emotional? Why do I have to ask them a hundred times to do something? How can they talk to me that way? Will they ever be able to handle a job or any responsibility? After I ask myself all those questions, and more, I remind myself that book stores are crawling with books on raising teenagers, so I must not be the only one worrying.*

*There is a great need to protect our teenagers from the world around them as well as from themselves. It baffles me why teenagers do not have better control of their impulses as if survival of the fittest would have corrected that human flaw by now. But until they are young adults, their brains are still developing and they will make decisions that could be harmful to themselves. They become more independent as they grow, fighting for their freedom, yet they need us now to guide and protect them as much as ever before. The difficulty in this is our children do not think they need us and they shut us out.*

*Breaking through the silence is difficult because many teenagers can be stubborn and they do not think we know what we are talking about. They are not always wrong about that accusation. Many times, parents talk but do not listen. We may hear our children, but we are not listening to them. We think we know what it is like being a teenager since we have all been one. However, as my wonderful friend Sheila enlightens me, "We may have been teenagers, but we have no idea what it is like to be a teenager in today's world."*

*At first, I thought this applied only to boys who go into their cave and not share any of their problems with us. My daughter, Olivia, shares so much with me I sometimes wished she had a cave, and my teenage son gives me the same answer to every question, "Fine." When talking to other parents, it seems to be an issue with both sexes in teenage years. In anticipation that one day my teenagers would shut me out, I did my best to begin dialog with them early and consistently. Every night I tried to lie down with each child and talk to them in the privacy of their rooms. I thought this gave them a safe place to open up to me and was hopeful this would continue into their teenage years. Nevertheless, what I have found is they stay up later than I stay up and they would rather be on Facebook or on the phone with a friend then lie down with me.*

*Getting teenagers to open up is not easy, and getting them to self-reflect and take responsibility can be almost impossible. But, these are all communication skills that are so valuable for them to ensure healthy relationships throughout their lives that communication skills must be taught just like teaching the ABCs. Unfortunately, schools do not have the budget to teach Feeling and Expressing Your Emotions 101, so the job falls solely on us.*

*Ah, the charm of raising teenagers - the moments you are not plagued with frustration are actually fun and exciting.*

# *Words and Actions from Barbara*

When recently reading the caption on the cover of a magazine, "Friends Don't Let Friends Stay Depressed," I thought about the challenge of respecting someone's wishes for privacy, and knowing when to step in; that point of equilibrium can be delicate. A few years ago a very dear friend was going through a divorce and "locked" herself away in her bedroom for over a year. I would call and call, but she would not answer. A group of us took turns going over and sitting with her and bringing by food. One of our friends would simply leave a meal on her doorstep and call her to let her know it was there. I was very close to her and being terribly concerned I finally got a little more assertive with her. At first I would bring her into the bathroom and have her brush her hair, then ask her to put on a little makeup before taking her for a ride, and eventually insisted we go out to lunch, a movie, or window shop. A friend can be trusted to intervene, to support, to listen.

- *Stay consistent with your calls. Being dependable creates an atmosphere of trust.*

- *Send a "Good Morning!" text every day. Try not to miss a day; do the best you can.*

- *You could use your cell phone to take pictures of the beautiful outdoors and send them off to brighten her day, especially if she is confined to the indoors.*

- *Sit quietly with your friend and listen or call and genuinely listen. Try not to interrupt. Take a cue if they want advice or conversation. When a person tells you about a problem or concern, they are not necessarily asking, nor ready, to hear your advice or "solution."*

- *Get them to go on a walk. If possible set up a regular time. If they ask about how you are doing, share your news, but do not burden them with your hardships. Unless you have shared the type of relationship that is deeply honest and you feel they want to hear the details and can cope with them. Sometimes it helps to empower friends who are not feeling in control of their own situation if you share a problem they can help you with.*

- *A troubled or ill friend may care about you, but they may be too vulnerable to absorb anymore difficulty; use your insight and best judgment.*

- *Make sure they are getting proper nutrition. People, who are in crisis mode, such as in a depression, or who are physically ill, need to adhere to certain practices: mindful eating, refraining from a high intake of sugar, alcohol and refined carbohydrates. A supportive program such as taking omega 3 supplements, vitamin D, Bs, chromium, calcium, magnesium, and other minerals, vitamins, and nutrients are essential to sustaining a healthy system, and even more essential for one that is stressed and depleted. These elements can be found in fresh whole food products; (many packaged foods often have high levels of sodium, preservatives, dyes and corn syrup, and should be avoided.) Fresh fruits, vegetables, fish, lean meats, (in moderation if you consume meat); will greatly support the distressed mind and body.*

- *Make sure your friend is getting at least eight hours of sleep plus daily, sunlight, and exercise. Try suggesting they practice relaxation techniques; practice together, as a temporary or long- term caretaker you likely need rejuvenation as well. Try biofeedback or yoga.*

- *Spending time in nature, and playing with a pet can help lower blood pressure, and raise levels of endorphins, (the "feel good" hormones), all this and sharing time with positive, comforting people increases a person's general feeling of well being. Ask other friends if they can rotate days with you to share the love, concern and responsibility.*

- *Keeping your thoughts and days activities, and aspirations, in a journal helps to provide a feeling of a measurable accomplishment. Bring her an attractive journal, and ask your friend to share her thoughts, she may want to keep it private; respect that decision.*

*Suggest she do something spontaneous, or novel; either alone, or better yet with a friend or a group of friends at first; sharing time with positive, comforting people increases a person's general feeling of well being.*

*Remember, if you are not a trained psychologist, and if you feel the depression, or the illness is severe and not improving, help them seek professional care.*

"It has been said that to be trusted is a greater compliment than to be loved; I can understand this.

With trust there is respect; without respect and trust there cannot be a genuine and abiding love"

- Barbara Lazaroff

# For You, I Wish
## My Love and Gratitude

*Life holds precious gifts for us, unfolding them as we call on them. All are treasures, yet there is one immeasurable in value to the heart. This gift is living within the essence of all women, regardless of age, or if she has given birth or not; the gift to nurture, to value, to bestow maternal love. I ask, but what is a mother? She is the one who lifts you when your heart is dragging, the one who finds you when you have lost you, the one who stands silent so you can sing. She cares for you in illness, celebrates you in triumph, and encourages you in hardship. You are my friend; when I am down, you lift me up, when I am lost, you find me, and when I achieve, you celebrate me. I wish for you my love and gratitude.*

"At all ages, our girlfriends offer us support and love,

whether our mothers are living down the street or

or are no longer with us... I am surrounded by loving women

who offer me the ability to be more loving,

and for that I am incredibly thankful."

-Tricia LaVoice

# Reflection

*It was early April last year when I was walking through the card section of Costco when the prettiest floral card caught my eye. I picked it up and began to read the beautiful devotion on the cover when I suddenly realized that it was a Mother's Day card. Quickly, I returned it to the shelf, trying to block out the sad feeling that overcome me when I accept that I am no longer able to mail my mother Mother's Day cards. But as I continued shopping, I could not stop thinking of the card, it was that pretty, and I thought about what it really means to send a Mother's Day card. That is when I decided to send a card to all the women in my life who had loved me, celebrated me, and stood still for me when I needed their support.*

*At all ages, our girlfriends offer us a special support and love, whether our mothers are living down the street or are no longer with us. I like to think about how women lived together in the beginning of time, in biblical times, and even now all over the world, in tribes. Together, they run villages, feed and nurture the children and men, attend to the sick and more, but they do it together, offering one another emotional support that replenishes them and provides the strength to continue giving to all who depend on them. In modern society, we are spread out, living separately in our own homes, raising our own families, but that does not mean that the bond between women is any less important. I used to worry that I gave too much time to my friends when we lived in Los Angeles. Although I was with my children the majority of the time, I would be talking with my friends, engaged in conversation while the children played. At school events, I worried that I socialized more than I paid attention to the events at hand. So when we moved to the quiet suburbs of Connecticut, I thought the isolation with my children would be good for my family. It was not. As I took care of their needs, I came to find that without the girlfriend lunches, the girlfriend walks on the beach, and the shared cups of tea, I was tired and cranky. Once, when I was complaining to a friend that I was lonely living in Connecticut, she asked, "How could you be lonely? You are surrounded by kids and a loving husband." I did not bother to defend myself, for I knew she had never had the experience of moving to a town devoid of close girlfriends and, therefore, could not appreciate what I was feeling. I did adjust to being in Connecticut without my friends, but I think my whole family will agree that it was not until I opened myself up to meeting new friends, to walk and talk and drink tea with, that I returned to my whole, happy self.*

*That year, I sent a Mother's Day card to a couple of special women who have always been maternal in their love to me, always making sure I am taking care of myself. I sent a card to my mother-friends of all ages to give them support and to thank them for their support. I sent one to each of my sisters, one to my mentor, and I sent one to my girlfriends who never gave birth but were just as loving in their friendship. Although I am not able to send my mother a card on Mother's Day, I recognize that I am surrounded by loving women who offer me the ability to be more loving, and for that I incredibly thankful.*

# *Words and Actions from Barbara*

Try demonstrating gestures of love more often; people need to connect on a more human level, particularly in this era of ever-increasing technology. My mother's fondest gifts from me as a child were not purchased, but rather created with my heart, mind and hands: an anniversary poem I composed and painted on a rock, a Mother's Day prose, "Beauty, My Mother's Glowing Face," that hangs on the kitchen wall, (no matter how many times they have moved), the albums of my sons' births, their beloved grandsons! My parents adore the videos, and the endless weekly photos I sent them of their grandsons as they grew, allowing them to "see" the boys mature from across the country. Some of my most valued possessions include cards my boys wrote and illustrated, and their drawings and clay work from school, all of which I recognize as masterpieces! Most precious are my tender memories of their hugs, kisses and deliciously unabashed words of affection and abiding love. Some of the most significant moments are how we always said, "I love you", when my sons and I would speak to my mom and dad on the phone. Since they have moved nearby there is never a "Goodbye" without an "I love you." My beau never ends a call without expressing love, and when we are apart, he calls me often for no other reason than to say the words.

- *The spoken word is the greatest gift. Just say how you feel. Think about the joy and comfort your friend and family receive from your warm words. If you are not naturally an expressive person, try practicing words of love and support; you may feel awkward at first, however, the positive rewards of closer relationships will ease that initial self-consciousness.*

- *Handwrite a letter of appreciation. Try to include details about their loving nature and their gift of friendship.*

- *Take pictures of their garden or yours, a family pet, their children, a car they are proud of, a funny or memorable moment from your friendship; frame them, or make greeting cards with the images. Although I never go anywhere without my camera, these photo-cards are Tricia's specialty! She has photographed every variety of rose bush in my garden and sends me notes on the cards she makes. She feels I don't take enough time to enjoy my roses.*

• *Bring over flowers for no other reason than to cheer her day.*

• *Simply make your friend a cup of tea or a sandwich and spend a little time sharing; these little acts of kindness nourish the soul, both for you and your friend.*

• *If you are seeking a grander gesture than flowers, arrive with a small tree and plant it together. You can research on the internet, or at the library, the symbolism behind a specific tree to help you make a meaningful selection. For example, Tricia sent me a Western Redbud tree which blossoms in springtime with purple flowers, which is my favorite color. This tree has unique heart shaped leaves which she felt represented our devoted friendship. She included lovely words that were soothing and uplifting. Her creative gift is timeless, and I was extremely touched.*

"The loneliest woman in the world is a woman

without a close woman friend."

- George Santayana, A Man of Letters

True, and written by a man no less!

When I was nine years old I composed this
for my mom as a Mother's Day gift.

## *Beauty, My Mother's Glowing Face*

*Beauty is a flower with dew on every petal,*
*Where bees who gather honey may pick this place to settle.*

*Beauty is a meadow, a flawless paradise,*
*One place God meant for everyone;*
*For beauty has no price.*

*Beauty is someone to love, someone to stand beside;*
*Who with you, would walk the earth,*
*Or cross the ocean wide.*

*Beauty is innocence,*
*intelligence,*
*And grace;*
*But most of all, beauty is,*
*My mother's glowing face.*

*Love, Barbara*

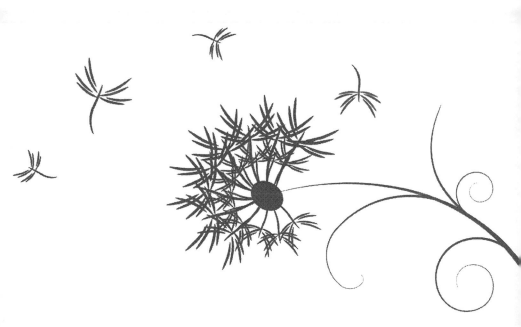

# For You, I Wish
## The Village Well

*There is a well where the children go to quench their infinite thirst; their thirst for love and safety, patience and acceptance; their endless needs for confidence, reassurance, direction, trust, and respect. This well I speak of I call "You." A hole below the surface of the earth or a spring bursting with purity - no matter what you call it, it is you who is responsible to gather the strength to quench the boundless thirst of your young. Some days your water overflows with abundance, yet on other days your well runs dry. Like the water that sustains their young bodies, the water from your well is essential to their being. There are no days off and the children, young and old, are not yet understanding or required to replenish what they take. So where do you go, what do you do when the depth and quality of your well water run short? Thankfully, wells are meant to be shared by all in the village. When you tire, let your children come to my well. When I tire, welcome my children to yours. Together, we can serve all those in need. For you, I wish the village well.*

"I can think of no more beautiful gift a friend can give to another friend than to love her children and help make a positive difference in their lives."

– Tricia LaVoice

# Reflection

*Extended family is a wonderful source of love and support to help promote a child's self esteem, build character, and instill values. But in today's world, many of us do not live close to our extended families. My family and Rich's family are very supportive of our kids; however, throughout most of our married lives, we have not lived near either of our families. We have therefore found ourselves relying on friends for added support.*

*Like the wish says, "There are no days off." The day I found out I was pregnant with Olivia, our first child. I became a mother; feeling vulnerable and responsible. From that moment on, in everything I did, I thought of her first. I remember that day and think about how many days I have had off from that responsibility since the day she was born, and I keep coming up empty-handed. Sure, we can go away on vacation or just out for the night, but no matter who we leave in charge – our parents, our best friends, or even the Super Nanny – we never stop being the mommy - the one they will call if there is a problem, the one they want if they are scared or need loving. We never stop loving and worrying about them. We may get a break from dinner and bedtimes every now and then, but emotionally there are no breaks.*

*I love nothing more than being the mother, the mommy, but there are days that I just do not have the emotional energy to be parenting the way I want to be parenting. There are some days I just want to yell, "Because I said so!" and I do. The boys will respond to my unwarranted yelling, but it seems to backfire on me with Olivia. I can yell at her five days in a row to clean her room to no avail, but if I speak softly while acknowledging that I understand it is not fun, yet would she please pick up her room, she will get to it much sooner and without the drama. On the days that I am tired and become reactive in my parenting instead of proactive, I greatly appreciate help from my closest friends with my children. Helping one another out with car-pooling, sleepovers, or dinner is an essential part of tag team mothering. However, going that extra step, being actively involved with one another's children, can make all the difference.*

*Barbara knows how irritable I can become when helping my children with their math homework. Many times, on the days Barbara picked my kids up from school, I would find her sitting with one of them, doing math homework.*

*And then there are the talks that kids seem to pay more attention to when they come from an adult other than their own parents. My heart melts when I hear one of my friends asking my children about their hobbies or school. The children seem to glow upon feeling the interest of another adult and eagerly share their thoughts and stories. Recently, Leeza sat with Olivia to talk about a future in journalism. I watched as Olivia took in every word, and I found myself reveling in and appreciating the way Leeza's love and friendship was making a difference in my daughter's life.*

*Mothering is the most rewarding job a woman can have, yet it is not always easy. I can't think of a more beautiful gift a friend can give to another friend than to love her children and help make a positive difference in their lives.*

# *Words and Actions from Barbara*

The next time you find yourself about to say, "Let me know if I can be of help," stop, reflect, and truly extend yourself by spontaneously doing just that; Act! Remember the precept, "The smallest act of kindness is worth more than the grandest intention." Mothers must support one another, and we understand so intimately other mothers' issues.

"It takes a whole village to raise a child" - African proverb. It takes a community of women to support each other so we can uphold our never-ending commitment to love and our obligations.

- *If you are going somewhere, offer to take a tired mom's child along with you.*

- *Help a friend's child with their homework, read to them, or ask them to read to you. I have done this often with friends and it is always deeply appreciated. (This is where I have stepped in for Tricia numerous times). I have actually learned and re-learned a great deal myself, (patience, as well as history, math, an interpretative review of Shakespeare, and a realization that I have forgotten a great deal of my years of university level chemistry and biology, and I'm embarrassed to admit some of my elementary school grammar!)*

- *Offer to host a friend's child's birthday party. One of my fondest memories was creating an English garden tea party for Tricia's daughter Olivia's thirteenth birthday. My garden is a gorgeous faux English mélange of aromatic flowers and trees. The young ladies dined on scones and clotted cream, little finger sandwiches, and decadent desserts. The beautiful table décor were composed of roses I cut and arranged from my garden, and all the girls wore hats! You can simplify this and the girls will still have a grand time! Be imaginative, have the ladies create hats from cardboard boxes, wrapping paper and ribbons, award a few prizes for the silliest, strangest, loveliest, and most dramatic creations. An indoor tea party with petite individual flowers, perhaps tiny tea roses that the girls can each take home would thrill them.*

- *When calling a friend's house, talk to her child about school and sports. Express genuine interest. When you discover their passions, suggest an outing; perhaps you know an expert in that area, a scientist, an actor, a professor, a doctor, an attorney, a talent agent, film maker, chef, businesswoman, an athlete that they could meet or exchange a letter or email with for inspiration.*

- *Consider taking a friend's child on your family vacation or over night to give her a respite. Last year my girlfriend was undergoing chemotherapy and wanted her son to enjoy his spring break; although we would miss sharing the annual trip with her, it was my profound joy to take her son, (who is good friends with my younger son), along for the vacation. This gesture eased her greatly, and she could concentrate on her health.*

- *If permitted, attend a school conference or doctor's appointment for your friend's child when she truly cannot make these important appointments and needs the extra support.*

- *Attend a school function, like Grandparent's Day, for a friend's child if they do not have grandparents living in the area, or they have passed away. This is something I would do almost every year for Tricia's children since her parents are both deceased. When my parents were in town, they would attend and be the "elder friends."*

- *Help your friend's child make a special birthday surprise or Mother's Day gift for their mother. Thank you Tricia for all the terrifically clever surprises you created with my sons to delight me, make me laugh, and help them feel great about their demonstrations of love.*

"Many people will walk in and out of your life, but only true friends will leave footprints on your heart."

- Eleanor Roosevelt, Former First Lady

# For You, I Wish
## My Care

*I walked in the weather today feeling the soft droplets of rainfall on my grateful face. A rain, a weeping of the sky releasing months of matter held high in the clouds until she can hold back no longer. I welcomed her downpour, for Mother Nature has worked diligently, turning the hardships of winter into a rainbow of color for those she loves. She is most deserving of a let down...I thought of you as I walked. I heard your concerned voice ask me, "Who takes care of you, my friend?" You place kudos on my doorstep and show appreciation for my words. Then you move to the next in need and place your arms there. Before retiring, you reach for one more weary soul, finally retreating to your own dwelling, where children await for their share of your love and affection. The role of the caretaker, the concierge to their world, squeezed between the young and the old, responsible for generations past and present filled with rewards, yet not getting easier with age. Now I ask you, my friend, who takes care of you? Are the clouds behind your eyes filled to capacity, wanting their own downpour? Do you fear letting go and flooding those you love? I watch you turn the hardships of your world into rainbows of color. I watch you nurture those young and old, care for the generations past and present. I wake to my world some days with the arms of an octopus, other days with clouds behind my eyes ready to burst, but if you can take my love, my friendship, my loyalty, rain or shine, I reach my hand to you in care. For you, I wish my care.*

"Who takes care of you my friend?"

- Tricia LaVoice

"Sometimes all we need is a good cry and just a little love."

–Tricia LaVoice

# Reflection

*Who takes care of you?*
*I asked this question to five of my closest friends and got a variety of an-*
*swers. Sadly, one of them, whom I have known forever and talk to every*
*day, replied, "@#%\* NOBODY." I think that was a message that I needed*
*to pick her up some groceries and take her kids for the weekend. I loved*
*Barbara's answer because I watch her try to save the world, so when she*
*replied with multiple names, I was pleased. She also has the most devoted*
*"manfriend" (she hates the term "boyfriend") a woman could ask for, and*
*wonderful, loving parents.*

*However, my exhausted friend above, as with many of my friends, has*
*teenagers she is raising and now aging parents who need her support,*
*and is going through a divorce. My parents were both in their mid-fifties*
*and healthy when they died – they were still in the giving seat. I have not*
*experienced the sandwich stage, but I watch my friends as they juggle the*
*roles of mothering children and being a caretaker for aging parents. It is*
*a stage that most mothers experience, and if we think back to when we*
*were young, we can remember our mothers caring for our grandmothers.*
*Unfortunately, women no longer gather around the fire and share respon-*
*sibilities, supporting one another while the men hunt. Most of us, regard-*
*less of whether we're taking care of parents or family or work or friends,*
*understand how overextending ourselves can build up and make us feel*
*like the tree in The Giving Tree, just like an old stump with nothing more*
*to offer than for someone to sit on us.*

*I wrote this Wish for Leeza two years ago when she was going through a*
*divorce and her mother was still alive with Alzheimer's. She is always so*
*kind to me and is always asking me who takes care of me. Yet, I watch her*
*give and give and give, desperately trying to lessen the burden of this ter-*
*rible disease on other families by setting up homes where caretakers can*
*gather to receive love and support. Like many women, she gives all day,*
*only to go home to give all night. Yet Leeza, like Barbara, gives so much*
*of herself to others, that she is too busy to realize the buildup behind her*
*eyes. She told me that when she read this Wish on her BlackBerry after*
*dropping her son off at school, she had to pull over and let herself cry.*
*Sometimes all we need is a good cry and just a little love and we can keep*
*going until the clouds fill up again and we need another letdown.*

*What I have learned from some of my friends, whose children are grown and off on their own and whose parents have passed, is how much they miss this stage in life and how quickly it all passes. They plead with me to enjoy every minute of it and tell me sad tales of an empty, lonely house. I try to remember this when I am feeling like an old stump, only good for sitting, but it is not always easy to talk yourself out of depletion. Sometimes a good cry clears my thoughts, or sometimes it is the love of a friend or the love of my husband. The best gratitude of all for the caretaker, however, is the sound of a child saying "Thank you" that does the trick.*

"We ascend from a long and noble tradition of sisterhood,

and the primitive need to bond, share,

and get along to survive."

–Barbara Lazaroff

# *Words and Actions from Barbara*

I have always believed it is our duty as women, and as "sisters," to help our tribe; both less and more experienced, both strong and frail, stride the challenges of life's path. There are so many pitfalls and mysteries in finding contentment, and although these women cannot live their lives vicariously, and we cannot protect them, (or ourselves), from all disasters, we can certainly instruct and offer alternatives to behaviors, actions, directions, words, life patterns that are less than effective. We can attempt to provide a bit of a cushion for their falls, or a springboard for their advancements. It is natural and sensible then that historically many cultures have demonstrated women gathered together working communally for the good of all. They labored side by side raising, feeding, and protecting each other's children and the home site, as men went off to hunt. We ascend from a long and noble tradition of sisterhood, and the primitive need to bond, share, and get along to survive.

- *Think broadly; utilize one of your talents to help others. Can you paint, sing, play an instrument, or otherwise entertain someone or make them laugh or smile? Reflect on what abilities you have that can be a powerful tool to aid others.*

- *Can you cook, sew or bake? Dance or draw? Teach a friend. I have a friend who is going to teach me how to knit.*

- *Are you skilled at accounting or good with technology? Perhaps you could help organize a friend's finances, or documents, and then instruct them how to do continue to do so themselves.*

- *Offer to fix a computer problem, or make a compilation of soothing music, or paint a wall, or a do a load of wash.*

- *Go over to a friend's home when she is too depressed to get out of bed, because you know that getting her up and out is vital. If she is physically ill, tidy up the home.*

- *Visit someone who has lost a loved one, not just in the first week or month, but well beyond when the reality of the loss is becoming cemented into their everyday life.*

• *Remind her: You must always believe in your ability to grow and learn, no matter how bleak the circumstances might seem.*

• *Ask your friend how you can specifically help her.*

"Call it a clan, call it a network, call it a tribe, call it a family:

Whatever you call it, whoever you are, you need one."

- Jane Howard, Author

"Well behaved women rarely make history."

– Laurel Thatcher Ulrich, Author

"Create a history and legacy you can be proud of; gather together, do not deceive, do not yearn, but rather earn your place of dignity. Speak truth, engage in honest actions, change what must be changed."

– Barbara Lazaroff

# For You, I Wish
## The Strength to Love

*I want to wish you something, but I am too exhausted to tend to my own needs, much less the needs of others. I feel as if I have given myself close to depletion in the absence of appreciation. I sit here with my pen, yet no words come to mind. Why then, if I feel so drained, do I feel such a need to reach out and wish for you tonight? I have read that both the receiver and the giver of acts of kindness benefit equally. Maybe my needs are self-serving. I try hard to get to a place in my life where I give without expectations or needing anything in return. True giving must come unconditionally. Tonight, I relapse. Therefore, I look to nature, one of our greatest teachers. I wonder if the ocean ever says, "I don't want to make waves today or provide food and oxygen for the marine world." Does she tire? And the sun, does he ever complain about shining? No matter where you are, what continent, country, or town, if you are sitting on the beach or walking through a forest, the sun is there. He does not care if you are young or old, rich or poor, black or white. You do not even have to be ethical and he will still shine on you. As you look directly to the sun, you feel a direct relationship, a beam of heat and light connecting you to him. He makes you feel as if for that moment, you are the only living thing on this earth he is caring for. His warmth surrounds you and you forget that hundreds of miles away, a cornfield is being nourished by his giving, and another hundred miles away, a child in the ghetto is being warmed. That is how I want to love. Tonight, when I seek love, I want the strength and goodness to love; so all those around me feel as if they are the only person on this earth I love at that moment. I am tired and have little poetry for you, but I have a wish for you. I wish you all my love and I wish you the strength to love all with all of your love. Some days it is all we have to give, and everyday it is all we really need.*

"I want the strength and goodness to love; so all those

around me feel as if they are the only person

on this earth I love at that moment."

– Tricia LaVoice

# Reflection

*I considered removing this Wish from the mother collection because it was not very uplifting, so I wrote the reflection below and set it aside. Then while in the process of finishing this book, I got a call from an old friend who is now a single parent trying to start her own business. She has no family nearby and works so hard at home she rarely has time for friends. When she called, she was hysterical, feeling horrible as a mother who had no love to give her child and no patience to let him make mistakes. I asked her who loves her. Who rejuvenates her heart with love and support so she can love and support him, obviously no one? This Wish is raw and honest, but talks to the hearts of all mothers. If you are fortunate to have a strong support system, I salute you. If you are not, I cannot stress the need to build one. As the flight attendant always says, put your own oxygen mask on first before assisting others. And yes, as part of her support system I did take her son for the weekend so she could rest. She would do the same for me, I am sure of that.*

*If there is a mother or caretaker out there who has not experienced the emotion of feeling nearly depleted and unappreciated, please write me and tell me your secret. Although many moments as a mother are full of love and appreciation, there are many times I find myself so tired I do not know where the strength will come to continue with dinner, homework, and bedtime. On these nights, I go into robot mode getting the job done without much emotion and the little emotion I do have certainly does not lead itself to patience and kindness. My father would say babies cry when they got tired, letting everyone around them know they need rest. While it is not socially acceptable for an adult to start crying every time they feel tired, we still feel miserable like a baby needing a nap.*

*It would be wonderful if we could all love without expectations of being equally loved back, if we could give unconditionally, if we never tired. But as the adults in the parent-child relationship, we are the givers, the providers, the ones with the open arms. Yet, we are humans and will make mistakes, tire, complain at times, indulge in self-pity, and simply want to be appreciated for our hard work. That is why when I wrote this Wish I was not wishing a mother the strength to love in order to benefit her family. I was really thinking about the mother herself. Knowing if she had the strength to love, she would feel appreciated and rested. When I feel so worn out from life, longing to be loved and valued, I crave to love like the sun, to never tire, to be so filled with love I warm the hearts of people near and far, but that is not possible. When I am feeling tired and unappreciated, I have little to give the children, even less for my husband, and, certainly, nothing left for me.*

*These are the nights I long to check my inbox and find an encouraging email waiting from a loving friend or two. Many times, I find one with a friend checking in or someone asking about getting together. However, the nights I do not find an email waiting I send one instead, believing this friend must need to feel loved too. Interestingly, giving back to another caretaker can help lift one's spirits. It is reassuring just to read someone asking, "How are you?" I have found this simple act of kindness to replenish the love temporarily absent from my heart, and I wish it to replenish the love from another loved one's exhausted soul too.*

*As mothers and caretakers, we will tire, we will make mistakes, all of us, but if we are doing the best we can at that moment, we are doing just fine.*

# *Words and Actions from Barbara*

"I am so tired I cannot even see ...yet I am too tired to fall asleep. I am thinking about how to resolve things, how to get my work done, help my boys, my parents."

These are my words from an email I sent to Tricia one night. How does this happen? As mothers, our job is never done and many times we find ourselves depleted. In these times, a friend can be a life saver. We must extend ourselves to each other to avoid getting too tired to enjoy our lives. For your "mother friends:"

- *Make or purchase dinner, (preferably not fast food), for her family once a month, or you can rotate within a group of friends and each cook dinner one night a week thereby creating a "Cook Free" number of nights. You will benefit as well!*

- *Just say out loud, "I think you are a wonderful mother!" And "I am so proud to be your friend." You can also be specific about what you find admirable about her, you are so: creative, patient, kind, humorous, wise, and organized. I adore the quote, "Women are great leaders, because we are always dealing with three children and two cookies!" We are the CEO's of our home, and some of us women are out in the workplace as well; we must help each other with the greatest and most important executive position in the world, raising healthy, productive, educated, and caring young adults. The environment and peace on this planet depends on the quality and character of our future generations. A dynamic child begins with a positive, well intentioned, attentive mother.*

- *Give her a candle, some bubble bath and a peaceful CD. It will offer her a sense of calm.*

- *Surprise her and stop by with her favorite, (healthy) snack, but if you find her at an inconvenient time, drop it off with a hug and leave.*

- *Help her rearrange furniture, or plant in the garden or hang pictures, or reorganize a cabinet.*

- *When she is going through a hard time, treat her to a casual dinner and a movie. If she loves the ocean or the mountains, but rarely takes the time to enjoy them, drive her there so she can go for a walk, relax and delight in the views. Ask a few friends to come along to share the experience.*

- *Use the mail to brighten her day. Keep mail supplies at your house to make it easy to just ship a simply token of love off with little effort. Mail her favorite candy, (or something healthier!), or a box of tea bags with a note saying, "Sharing a moment with you, remember I am there in spirit."*

- *If you can afford it, send her for a massage, perhaps the tribe can all contribute. You might try to do the massage yourself. (One of my dearest friends was hospitalized and we all took turns massaging her feet! Some of us had more natural talent than others, but we were all appreciated.)*

- *Once when I was not feeling well I had a "mother- friend" who came to my home every evening for a week to walk my dogs and close up the house for the night. In return, I took her children for the weekend and she and her husband had some much needed time alone. There are countless ways for mothers to support one another.*

"The house does not rest upon the ground,

but upon a woman."

– Mexican proverb

"I sometimes I feel I cannot find another ounce of strength

to do anymore that day; until I see one of my sons',

or a  dear friend's face smile, or cry, or ask for help."

– Barbara Lazaroff

# For You, I Wish
## The Chance to Observe Like a Student

*I observed like a student of art devouring a museum piece as he brought you the loveliest of his paintings, but you sent him away, demanding more. He entered again holding his best work, his shoulders broad, his smile long, but the measuring stick you held was gauged for others and he fell short. With a head hung low, he promised greatness and returned to his work. I saw delight in your eyes, heard you boasting of his talent as you felt sure your frustration pushed him to his best. Again he entered, this time a bit unsure; you saw excellence yet asked for perfection. Then and there, I observed like a student of art devouring a museum piece, his epiphany that he would never be enough in your eyes, never live up to your expectations, so in survival mode, he held his shoulders broad, his smile long, and returned to his work, never needing your approval again. For you, I wish the chance to observe like a student of art devouring a museum piece.*

"Our intentions lose their meaning if our children's interpretations are different than what we are trying to convey."

– Tricia LaVoice

# Reflection

*I was asked to write this Wish by a friend of mine who was very upset about the relationship her son had with his father, her ex-husband. She said her son confided in her that he never felt he was good enough in his father's eyes and that no matter what he did, his father found fault with him. My friend was concerned this was affecting her son's self-esteem, and she was very frustrated. She asked me to write something that she could share with the father to hopefully open his eyes. As is often the case with writing, I had to put the thought on the back burner until the Wish came to me. But as I wrote the Wish, I felt I was being somewhat unfair. I knew this father well, and I knew that he loved his son very much. I knew he was very proud of his boy, and many times he had told me great things about his son. I also knew the father thought he was doing his son right by pushing him, and he believed it is a father's responsibility to prepare his son for the world. My friend was grateful for the Wish, but she never gave it to her ex-husband. I was glad about that.*

*I think about all of us parents and the way we see ourselves versus the way our children see us. Just recently, Olivia saw a Wish I wrote on the home page of our local yoga studio. After reading it, she looked to me and said, "Wow, Mom, that was good, but I would think you would be a nicer person if you wrote stuff like that." I guess I took it as a compliment.*

*I believe that in our hearts we are doing our best for our children. I do, however, think we all need to reflect every once in a while and look at our parenting style through the eyes of our children. Are we complaining too much? Are we sufficient in celebrating their achievements? Are we harping on their failures? Have we truly given thought to what we really want for our children – for them to like themselves, for them to feel confident – and are we helping execute these goals?*

*All of us, including myself, could read this Wish and fail to spot ourselves in it. After speaking to her ex-husband about their son, my friend said she thought it was pointless to send the Wish. Her ex-husband saw her as being too lenient, and he felt just as strongly about the damage this leniency was doing to their son. Obviously, she disagreed with him. In my marriage, I know there are times when I feel that Rich and I are coming from two totally different points of view with the kids, and neither one of us is very open to seeing the other parent's viewpoint. Self-reflecting and recognizing our faults is difficult, but when it comes to the sensitive subject of parenting, it can be almost impossible. The issue here, though, is our children and how they see us as parents. Going to the source and having honest conversations with our children, allowing them to feel safe to speak their minds, may be the best way to truly understand the effects of our parenting. Ultimately, our intentions lose their meaning if our children's interpretations are different from what we are trying to convey.*

# *Words and Actions from Barbara*

There are many ways to help our children develop a positive self image; we must start by having healthy self-images as parents. Our children will look to us for signals regarding how we relate to the world around us, how we cope, what we determine to be a healthy successful happy life. Hopefully these are authentic values, not merely "success" that is measured in fame or monetary gain alone. In our quest to guide our children we must be careful not to project our expectations and hopes onto them for our own satisfaction, or self-aggrandizing purposes. Perhaps the family business is medicine, or in my case, design and the restaurant industry; I cannot expect my sons to follow in the family businesses. If they wish to do so, I will vigorously support them. However, my true hope is that they fulfill their own personal destiny. As parents we must be firm about good work study habits and character, however, we must refrain from excessively criticizing our children, forcing their life and career decisions to parallel ours, and remember to constantly show love and support.

- *Focus on the positive, and highlight your children's strengths.*

- *Work on improving their mastery in areas which they are less accomplished. Practice with them reading, throwing a ball, swimming, biking, mathematics, or art. Ask them what they would like help with. If you find you have conflicts when you try to teach your child, if you can afford it hire a tutor, or ask the school for additional help. There are also superb afterschool athletic programs, volunteer tutors, and community centers with a variety of programs that help cultivate proficiency in a broad range of areas.*

- *Make by hand an encouraging poster or plaque and hang in their room, or outside their bedroom door. I am a great believer in the influence of inspiring quotes.*

- *Randomly text them a message of pure love and encouragement.*

- *Invite your child to your room and ask them to sit down. Tell them how proud you are of them.*

- *Tell your child, "You do not have to be the very best at everything you desire at this moment, but if you strive to be better you will reach one or more of your goals and find deep satisfaction knowing your efforts were realized."*

- *Reward them for effort, not just accomplishment. We should always remember the fable of the tortoise and the hare: the hare was far too sure of himself and got lazy; he figured he did not need to keep a consistent pace, he could stop and catch up later, but the tortoise kept moving diligently along, and to everyone's astonishment beat the naturally speedy hare. However, if the tortoise hadn't won he still would have been a star as far as I'm concerned; I would recognize his faith in himself, his tenacity, courage and the sheer magnitude of his resolute effort.*

- *Pay attention to your speech. If you want to point out a behavior that requires adjusting, first express at least two things you feel your child has done which are positive. Wait a few minutes, let them enjoy the praise. Perhaps give them a hug. Then bring up the behavior you think they can improve on.*

- *Talk to your children about things that you needed to improve upon when you were young. Tell them how you felt when you failed at something. Reinforce what you discovered about yourself from those missteps, or disappointments; what you did to gain proficiency in those areas, and how those lessons guide you and prevent you from not repeatedly stumbling in similar situations.*

"Life is a grand canvas and you should

throw all the paint on it that you can"

- Danny Kaye, Actor, Dancer, Singer,

and Accomplished Amateur Chef

# For You, I Wish
## The Boy on the Couch

*I rushed from my bedroom to the kitchen, a million things to do. The corner of my eye caught a young boy sitting alone on the edge of the couch. I quickly called out to him, "You good?" "I'm good." I went about my chaos as if averting the end of the world by returning all phone calls, paying the bills, and picking up the laundry. I moved like a tire across a trail; the faster I spun, the less I caught in my treads. The boy the universe entrusted in me to guide and nurture called out from the couch, "Mom, you good?" I ask myself, "How long does it take to make a memory? How long does it take to make a difference? Three hours a day? One hour a day? Ten minutes here and there?" Think of your memories. I loved the trips to the shore, the nights out at the movies. However, my favorite memories are the ones ten minutes here and there, the walks around the block with my father, the quick cups of tea with my mother, listening to my big sister's stories about her day. These are the moments that molded my thoughts, instilled my values, tended to my self-worth. Remarkable that the right ten minutes can stay with us forever, making a lifetime memory. We cannot be expected to notice every new freckle dance across this boy's face, but ten simple minutes, the right minutes, can make a memory... I flew through the kitchen again, this time slower in pace, but my mind still raced. Then the realization that the world was not ending hit my brakes and stopped me in my tracks. I walked into the family room and looked at the kindness in my son's eyes, I felt the warmth of his hand as I took it in mine and I relished in the delight on his face when I said, "Come, let's take a few minutes and go outside to watch the world change."*

" How long does it take to make a memory?

How long does it take to make a difference?

Remarkable that the right ten minutes can stay with us

forever, making a lifetime memory."

- Tricia LaVoice

# Reflection

*I was pregnant with our fourth child when Rich and I were at a dinner party with some of the parents from Olivia's school. The woman hosting the party had two children herself, but came from a family of four. I remember so clearly her telling me that she felt she never received enough attention growing up and she hoped that by having two children herself, she would have the time and energy to give each child plenty of individual attention. I rubbed my big, bulging belly, feeling life move inside me, thinking, "What have I done? Can I be enough for each of them?" Then she offered me hope. She told me about how her mother would make an effort each night to lie down with each one of her children in their beds to make sure they all got alone mommy time each day. I thought, "Yes, I can do that."*

*Bills and responsibilities are a reality. We all have limited time for leisure, and I imagine we all wish we had more time and energy for our children. It is unfair to assume one mother has more time for her children versus another, based solely on the number of children she has. A mother of one can be less involved in her child's life than a mother of six. It all depends on the time and energy given. That is when the beauty of creativity comes into play. With just a little thought, we can turn everyday events into meaningful memories; with a little effort, we can make our children's worlds that much more beautiful to think back on.*

*There was another mother of four at our school who I would watch interact with her children from time to time. On field day, I would watch her as she walked with her daughter from one event to the next, as the rest of us moms hung together, chatting. She was creating a memory, knowing how happy her daughter was to have her mother's undivided attention as she competed in her events.*

*It is so important to give our children beautiful, meaningful memories from their childhoods because the time we take to make them is what helps define our children, building on their self- worth. My father used to say, No child asks to be born. So true, but how easy it is to get caught up in the hustle and bustle of life and forget to stop and make memories.*

*We did not have a lot of money growing up, but we had enough for a middle class American family to enjoy life. We took a yearly vacation to an island and had our weekly horseback riding lessons. I had a pretty Easter dress to wear each year and plenty of toys under the tree. However, what I remember most is lying on the couch at night, watching television with my mother, and the way she would scratch my scalp. I hated the weird noise it made inside my head, but I loved lying in her arms, so I never complained. I remember how she would let me in her room on Saturday nights and how I would watch her get ready to go out with my father for the night. She would play Dionne Warwick music and ask me how she looked while I danced in the mirror. Of course, there was not a more beautiful woman in the world to me. When she was gone, it was okay, I had my time, I had my memory. The little things that we make special, the things that do not take much time, just a little effort, can make all the difference in our children's lives.*

"Can I be enough for each of the them?"

–Tricia LaVoice

# *Words and Actions from Barbara*

The sweetest memories don't require anything but a little time, thought, creativity, and sometimes a childish sense of fun!

- *While driving play "Race the Moon". Watch how the moon follows you home, sometimes appearing way in the lead, and then falling far behind with a turn in the road. Also while driving, have the child close his or her eyes and try to guess where you are situated at that moment, or if they don't know the destination, ask them to guess where you are both going.*

- *Let each child pick what is served for dinner once a week.*

- *Go out on a "date" once a month, or more often, with each child separately. Perhaps a movie, dinner, a museum, the zoo, a planetarium, an aquarium, a sports event. Ask your child where they would like to go.*

- *During dinner play, "Who is Coming to Dinner?" Each family member gets to "invite" three people to the meal and must explain their selection: famous or not famous, from the past or present, real or fictional. (Assume all loved ones are already included.) As an added novelty, you can discuss whether your guests would approve of the food being served!*

- *Push the furniture back and have a family picnic somewhere in the house.*

- *Have a family sleepover party in the TV room. Roll out the sleeping bags or put the throw pillows out. Play board games, charades, get a karaoke machine and be silly!*

- *Make one night a week movie night and have the family sit together and watch a film. Have the children help you make popcorn and healthy snacks. Afterwards, that evening, or the next, discusses the film.*

- Read book series out loud; one that captures the attention of all the kids.

- Burn a CD of their favorite music and share it with them while you drive. Sing along if they are agreeable to the idea.

- If you have a home office, or projects you have brought home, have your child sit on the floor or across the desk from you. Tell them they are your co-worker today. Pretending to be at work with your child empowers them and fosters confidence. You can put a time-frame on this, if you need to concentrate. Give your child a task like sharpening the pencils, faxing, helping to copy information, let them feel like they are increasing your productivity. Compliment them, even if their presence causes little delays. When my older son Cameron was only six he started to sit at my drafting table and draw plans of an imaginary "The Most Perfect Restaurant Design in the World", and "His Dream House", which happily looked a lot like ours except one room was made completely out of pizza. (I have saved these, because they are priceless!) My biggest concern was making certain he did not fall off the drafting chair.

- Look at family photos and create a scrap book together for someone else in the family.

- Go together and pick out seeds and then plant them. Watch how wonderfully $1.99 can miraculously grow into something beautiful to smell or eat. Show a child how a potato can sprout, or an artichoke can produce a truly unusual flower.

- On the internet, or in the library, you will find fascinating and easy home science projects: Make a tornado in a bottle, a functioning potato or orange clock, or demonstrate how water and oil don't mix; explain the concept of density. Pour food dye into a vase with a flower and watch as the color rises up the stem and alters the color of the flower petals; then explain how plants get their nourishment. Experiments about magnets, gravity, light, and many more will fascinate your child. Depending on your child's age you can simplify the explanations or expand upon them. You will educate, as well as delight your child, as you share unforgettable moments together.

- For younger children make masks or costumes out of items already in the home. You can use shoe boxes, ribbons, and old sheets, pots for hats, tin foil, old clothes, newspapers and magazines. You can also create collages on paper, frames or serving trays, dioramas, window décor, (paper snowflakes are a classic favorite of mine), mobiles, and welcome signs for the front door.

- Prepare your child for a bubble bath with soothing music. Use battery operated candles for safety, unless you are present and the flame candles are not in reaching distance., This is a terrific way to provide your child with some relaxation time, particularly if they have trouble sleeping. Never leave young children alone in the bath; safety first, privacy is for older adolescents and young teens.

# For You, I Wish
## A River's Love

All an entire river knows is to journey home, letting nothing stand in her way. In times of drought, she flows with calmness, low to the ground, not rousing the earth. In times of surge, she roars, rapidly racing her course. Place an obstacle in her way and she will overcome it with her determination and spirit squeezing under, over, and around the largest of boulders, the smallest of debris. All she knows is to journey home. All I know is to love you, letting nothing stand in my way. In times of struggle, I will remain gentle, providing you clarity. In times of conflict, I will move swiftly, softening your ache. If you detach from me, I will tenderly wait. If you place an obstacle in my way, I will trounce it, and if you find resentment and fury with me, I will humble myself. All the river knows is to journey home, as all I know is to love you. For you, I wish a river's love.

"All the river know is to journey home,

as all I know is to love you."

–Tricia LaVoice

# Reflection

*The greatest gift we can offer our children is to love them unconditionally. It is the essential ingredient that allows them to grow and experience love with others throughout their lives. When children feel unconditional love, they learn to love themselves, to have loving friends, and to be a loving friend. It is the building block, stable and healthy, that allows them to be in loving relationships as adults and become loving parents themselves.*

*It is important that we do not take for granted the terms of unconditional love and that we verbally express it. Many children will not understand that they are loved unconditionally and will focus on their parents' expectations of good grades, achievement in sports, and good behavior. As parents, of course we want our children to achieve and to be happy, but we know we will love them just as much if they fail. We also understand that if one of our children struggles while the other achieves, this also does not affect how much we love our children. However, young minds are sensitive. It is important to explain to a child what unconditional love is and how you have loved him or her that way from the start and will until the end, no matter what happens along the way.*

*I have always told my children that I may not always like their behavior, but I always love them. Of course, as a mother of four, each one of my children has asked at one point or another which one of them I love the most, and my answer is always the same: Nature makes it impossible for me to love one of you more. As a mother, I am given endless love to love you all equally and without conditions. This usually quiets them for a while.*

*I have also found that as my children grow older and the teenage years begin to haunt and entertain our home, there are fewer and fewer opportunities to express my unconditional love to them. However, it is just as important to remind them of this love in the difficult teenage years as it ever was. Many times, when one of them is acting like a classic teenager and fighting me on an issue for no apparent reason then to argue, I have found that if I can muster the strength to throw out an I love you and only want the best for you (when what really I want to do is send them to live with an aunt), they calm down more quickly and hear me rather than fight me. Loving a child unconditionally is a blessing for both the child and the parent. I cannot think of anything more rewarding than a life filled with loving memories with your children. Barbara's mother, Ellie, is a beautiful example of a mother dedicated to her children from the start to the end. She has a maternal energy that is felt by all in her life. I love listening to her yell to Barbara as she walks out the door to be careful driving or when Barbara is sick, Ellie worries for her as if she were still her little girl. At 84, Ellie tells me all the time, "You never stop being a mother, Trish, but they grow so fast, so make sure you hug them and tell them every day how much you love them."*

*I really try to live by her words, hoping to have similar beautiful memories to hold when I am 84. However, what is much more important is that my children hold memories of being unconditionally loved when they are 84.*

"We strive to give our children a feeling of place in
the world by grounding them with home and family;
a heritage of belonging. If we have done a fine job, one day
they will soar off and find a place of belonging wherever life
may take them; because they carry home in their heart."
- Barbara Lazaroff

A tenet that has become truer as I have grown
more intuitive and aware:
"I've learned that people will forget what you said, people
will forget what you did, but people will never forget how
you made them feel."
– Maya Angelou, Poet and Author

# *Words and Actions from Barbara*

As a mother the most salient legacy you can imprint upon your children is the irreplaceable and powerful gift of acceptance and support; purely for being the people they are. Your "gift" of genuine and unconditional love possesses a matchless value. These are the memories that will carry them through their lives. Your love will have a far greater impact on your child than any video game or pair of shoes they once swore they could not live without.

- *If they are out of line, always tell your child it is their behavior that you are disapproving of, not them.*

- *While they are out with friends, send them a loving text.*

- *Randomly and often tell them, "I love you."*

- *Put notes in their lunch boxes. Be respectful of their privacy as they get older.*

- *Hug them. Physical affection is an important emotional connection.*

- *If they say mean things to you, refrain from saying them back. Remember you are an adult.*

- *Turn off your cell phone when you spend time with them. This lets them know you do not want to be disturbed because they are the most important people in your live.*

- *Frame their artwork and achievements and hang them on the wall or just tape them up on the refrigerator. Acknowledge their work more than once. Say, "Every time I look at your art I feel happy" or, "I am so proud of your report card, I love looking at it every day."*

- *On cold mornings, throw their clothes in the dryer for a few minutes and bring them to them while warm. Preheat the car before they come out to go to school.*

- *Walk in the rain together.*

# For You, I Wish
## The Lessons of Boyhood

*So the day has come when they call you a man, when all you have known is to be a boy. So how do you know how to be a man? By remembering everything you learned being a boy. If one person on the team breaks the rules, the game is ruined for the whole team. The go-cart you built in your garage with your best friend is a much sweeter ride than any you can buy at the store. The only time you should be in a box is when you are rolling down a hill. Climb the corporate ladder like you climbed a tree, never looking back or letting fear get in your way while avoiding the sap. Remember what you learned being a boy. Things that make your heart pound are worth doing twice. If it smells bad, it probably is bad. The best place to find safety in times of trouble is in a pair of arms. And like a game of tennis, it is better to serve than to be served. Life will flash like summer vacation; get to the beach, find love in a book, and visit with friends. Never forget what you learned being a boy when becoming a man, remembering the most important lesson of all: your legs will carry you on your journey, but your family will carry you on their backs. For you, I wish the lessons of boyhood.*

"Raising children who are compassionate and giving,

happens when we begin instilling altruistic behavior early;

Not by words alone, but by example and

clear and consistent actions."

– Barbara Lazaroff


"The understanding of atomic physics is child's play,

compared with the understanding of child's play."

-David Kresh, Poet

*Like many friends, Barbara and I became friends when our sons, Byron and Billy, became friends. Billy spent a lot of time over at Barbara's home, as Byron spent a lot of time at our home. Byron just slipped into place, as one of our own when he was at the house.*

*I wrote this Wish for Barbara's son, Byron, as he turned the wonderful age of thirteen. Fittingly, Barbara writes the reflection and actions to follow. Enjoy, Tricia*

# *Words and Actions from Barbara*

As parents, we are creating the future of our country and the world. Our children will be the next generation of leaders, voters, citizens and teachers. Several will be architects of buildings; others will build aircraft, while some of our children will be practitioners of medicine and law, artists, journalists, entertainers, or advocates for social change. All of them will influence each other, and the planet.

Childhood should be a time of joy and adventure, but equally a journey of growth, a time of learning to share, cooperate, compete, communicate, win with grace, and lose with equanimity. Children should learn to experience life's disappointments as opportunities to gather insight into ways they can become stronger and more diligent in their work efforts and relationships.

We want our children to recall a childhood filled with happy moments. However, childhood and the developmental years of young adulthood need to be structured with lessons in responsibility, organization, altruism, good family values, as well as instruction in good citizenship. These lessons need not always be somber and tedious. Creative and joyful ideas abound for guiding our children to be the best they can be!

As I was writing my thoughts on what I believe creates a well rounded and healthy young person, I started to realize that many of the virtues and character qualities I hold dear are the very values that my mom taught me. Surprisingly, those values and qualities are echoed in the guidelines I was asked to adhere to as a Camp Fire Girl, Brownie, and Girl Scout. I then reread the Boy Scouts of America's Oath, and these principles are indeed ones that we should hope our children, and we as adults, aspire to uphold.

We learn many of these lessons by watching the behavior of those around us, primarily our parents, if they are involved, loving, and compassionate people, we have a better opportunity to become fine citizens of the world. How we respond and cope with our triumphs and failures are often a reflection of how we have seen those we respect and love respond to these situations.

Although we often believe that our words should carry greater authority and profound meaning just because we're the parents, it is more often that we find our actions speak the loudest. Our children watch how we treat our spouses and other family members such as our elderly parents, to people who provide us with services such as those who bag our groceries, the attendant at the gas station, and the busboy in the diner.

They are aware at the youngest of ages how we interact with figures of authority, such as police officers and teachers. They hear and see how we behave in a traffic jam (do we yell, use profane language), and if we are curt, impatient, demanding, or demeaning to salespeople in a department store.  All these are lessons our child assimilates on a very primal level. We can  either produce  respectful, kind hearted, altruistic children who treat others with respect, or children who feel entitled and superior to those around them and who grow up to treat others with arrogance and disdain. The latter situation is a disastrous formula for developing and maintaining healthy, happy relationships that are genuine and not based on false grounding such as material acquisitions, status.

Another negative consequence of the indulged, haughty, undisciplined child is contempt for authority, which can lead to individuals who feel they are "above the law." We see a breakdown of marriage through adultery and poor communication. We watch in disbelief, (sadly we  are less surprised these days), as our heads of corporations and those allegedly committed to public service, even our clergy, violate our trust by committing crimes and engaging in immoral behavior that ends up in a free-for-all court battle or a jail sentence. We witness the devastation visited on those who trusted these "leaders of society", icons who eventually proved to be self-important and lacking true virtue.

Certainly, in time, our children start to consider emulating their peers. Therefore, our attention to their friendships is essential. We begin our important job as parents by working to instill character, a sense of community, purpose, compassion, a love of education, and a desire to live a life of purpose and value. How do we accomplish such a heady task and still raise a child with joy, filled with a childhood of happy memories?

If we are a consistent presence in their young lives, we have a better hope of producing young adults who have a strong sense of personal esteem and a powerful connection to family so that outside influences such as drugs, drinking, promiscuity, or simply poor work habits, and rude behavior do not have the powerful influence they do with children that feel less attached to family values. We do this as best we can, knowing we will make mistakes.

Divorce, an absent father, or mother, economic stresses, health issues, all affect our efforts. We know that we all meet with life's disappointments and that rather than try to protect our child from every stumble, these moments build character and create situations where our children learn to meet obstacles and develop techniques for problem solving, lessons they will need throughout life. Additionally, when we provide parameters of proper behavior toward others, respect, and caring for animals and all people, honoring their differences, and lastly, understanding to care for personal property, their own, as well as others, we develop young people who have a deep appreciation for their own bodies and minds and the rights of others. Profound understanding of the distinguishing lines of our place and rights in the world in relation to others is a complex equation, and often requires a lifelong series of lessons. The school my boys attended had a wonderful poster hanging in the halls. It said, "My rights end where yours begin."

Providing our children with love and responsibilities, a playground of imagination as well as a program of chores, and a youth of instruction in young adulthood is our parental balancing act. It takes infinitely more work as an involved parent to read with our children, make certain they are reading independently, check their homework, consult with their teachers, be aware of what they are looking at on the computer and watching on television, truly knowing their friends and their confidantes' parents, knowing where they go when they leave the house, and what they are doing when they get there, can be exhausting. It is far more effective however, than to just hope they are behaving and getting their work done. If you do not provide the groundwork of good work/study habits and discipline in childhood, don't expect it will be easy to instill these practices, or effectively dole out discipline much later on. The most important step in building a strong house is the foundation. Get it right; take the time and effort at the ground level, and the walls have a better chance of going up straight and enduring the battering of the changing times: the storms of life.

- *Storytelling is a wonderful way for a pre-reader to "read" to you! My sons and I had a couple of characters we would create stories around, (Pickles the Cat was a favorite). I would tell the first one, they would tell the next one, every night. This practice also teaches your children the fine art of listening, something, as adults, we need to constantly enhance.*

- *Read to your children every day, or ask someone in your home to do so when you are not available. A grandparent, a friend, an older sibling. Reading promotes the importance of education and is one of the important tools for excelling in school. Education is the vehicle for a life of choices with regard to work and fulfilling dreams.*

- *Explain to your children that even after they graduate, continuing to educate yourself is an important practice and truly a luxury. I have a girlfriend who took an art history class and an Italian class with her son. Whatever field you are in, you can always learn more.*

- *Display words of inspiration and guidance in your children's rooms, or place them in your child's lunchbox every day. (As your child matures, they will likely want this practice to stay at home!)*

- *I think every parent and child should read IF by Rudyard Kipling. My beau read this poem to my son at his Bar Mitzvah; you can adjust it to relate to a young lady as well. Each line is a gem, speaking to the virtues of patience, honor, perseverance, dignity, honesty, forgiveness, humility and more; a few lines follow:*

"If you can keep your head when all about you;
Are losing theirs and blaming it on you;
If you can trust yourself when all men doubt you"

The poem also speaks to the virtue being above lies and hatred, walking with kings and the common man alike, and relating to both. It also speaks about aspirations without losing sight of reality or allowing your passions to rule neither your reasoning, nor your thinking, without action, be your goal.

"If you can dream, and not make dreams your master,
If you can think, and not make thoughts your aim."

We must learn to cope with success and failure, and understanding that both have more in common than we realize. Living with humility, as opposed to false pride about our good fortune, and alternatively not being destroyed, or believing in our complete demise with regard to situations that do actualize, is the key to a life of equilibrium and the definitive mark of a man, (or a woman), of distinctive character.

"If you can meet with Triumph and Disaster
And treat those two imposters just the same;

The poem celebrates an individual who can bear witness to his life's work being destroyed, and gather the strength to rebuild yet again; a person who respects people, but not unduly impressed by anyone, a man of both daring and quiet dignity. The final lines sum up with the sage advice of filling every minute of your existence with purpose, and giving life everything you have within you; each minute is finite, when it passes it is gone forever; all of the aspects of character referred to in IF are the making of a boy into a man.

"If you can fill the unforgiving minute
With sixty seconds' worth of distance run,
Yours is the Earth and everything that's in it.
And, which is more; you'll be a man, my son!"

Not surprisingly the Boys Scouts of America's Oath highlights adherence to similar virtues:

They are trustworthiness, loyalty, helpfulness, friendliness, courtesy, kindness, obedience, cheerfulness, thriftiness, bravery, cleanliness, and reverence.

The motto of being prepared and the slogan to do a good deed every day are habits and actions we should all work to achieve. Whether your child is male or female, is a member of the Scouts, or another club, or none at all, this Oath is a terrific guideline to post!

Here are other ideas for building character in your child, or helping someone else's child, as well as learning to parent more creatively and effectively:

- *Have your child write one quote, dream, or aspiration that they have read, or that they create themselves, and either have them keep a journal, or post them on a board! Perhaps not just in their room, maybe everyone could take a turn to post the best quote of the day on the refrigerator, or the official "Idea Board."*

- *There are many excellent books about raising good children. Read them; discuss them with friends, your parents, and counselors.*

- *Join a parent support group. Seek guidance if you feel you need comrades. We all do. Some mothers do not have family or friends nearby on which they can rely. They may have to find other informed and concerned groups.*

- *If you are aware of a child that could use some adult companionship, a Big Brother or Big Sister organization is something you can suggest to the busy mom or dad. If the dad is not in the home, often boys would do well to have a Big Brother or a male role model, such as an uncle or family friend. My boys do not have a father in the home; although they occasionally dine or go skiing together, the day to day interaction is missing, and so important. I think having male tutors for them was a good choice. Often after completing their work, the guys would go out and throw a ball around, compose music, or simply talk. Now there is a man in my life that relates to them and rides a bike with my younger son, has taken my older son to a shooting range, taught* one son to weld, the other to fish. Parents cannot be replaced but there are ways to add role models, and adult pals into your child's life. Young girls need mothers, (and dads), if there is a young lady you know whose mom is deceased, or not in the home, or works long hours, offer to provide some "girl-time", those moments of bonding are vital to developing a positive, secure sense of self and sisterhood. Take her to your office or to afternoon tea, get a mini-makeover together, or go rollerblading. I have devoted time, resources and heart to an organization that is a safe haven and school for abused teenage girls; I truly benefit as much as they do.

- The children your children are friends with does matter, and having communicative relationships with those parents is important. Sincerely work on that. Have them over, or bring a cake and visit their home. Explain that you would like get to know each other and discuss your principles and beliefs, and the rules you expect your own children to live by. This can sometimes prove to be amusing, many times I experienced one of my children saying, "But his parents let him do that!" When I would compare notes with the other parents, we would have a good laugh because it was always a hopeful tale. Some parents are more interested in the social and economic standing of their children's friends than the more far more important issue of shared values and parenting style; don't make the mistake of confusing status with substance.

- Be firm, but not inflexible. You need to constantly re-evaluate your parenting decisions depending on the age, and responsibility quotient of each of your children. Communicate with the other parents. Remember; your child will try the renowned, "So-and-so's parents say it is okay!" Have parent and kid get-togethers and play dates. Factors, such as the rules, moral expectations, and educational study styles should matter to you exceedingly more than the race, religion, or ethnic backgrounds, or financial status of your children's friends. Your children will be part of a global experience when they mature. The more they learn, the greater they will understand the importance of accepting and respecting other peoples' customs. I know the times my children have traveled, not only abroad, but also within America, they have greatly furthered their understanding of how other people live, *which will serve them well as future world citizens.*

- *If you cannot afford to travel there are books and videos that open your child's mind up to the rest of their global community. This is so vital in educating your children, particularly if you live in very homogenous areas with little diversity. Reciprocally, children that live in urban areas sometimes deal with racial and ethnic tension. Children's museums, as well as school and library programs sometimes speak to these issues, both for children, (who tend to be more tolerant), as well as adults, (who sometimes negatively influence their children with ingrained prejudices and misconceptions). Some children never see other areas of their own city. Explore with your child, bring a group of parents and children, and discuss the cultural diversity. The children and adults can make drawings, or shoebox dioramas, or write poetry of short stories regarding what impressed or surprised them the most*

- *Start instilling altruistic behavior early. Take your kids to a shelter or do as my friend did every Saturday, she and her twin daughters packed brown bags with food for the hungry; they did this for ten years!*

- *Teach your children to save a bit of whatever they earn, or receive as an allowance, and share a bit with those less fortunate. If your children get an allowance, have them set aside at least ten percent every week for a charity of their choice and at the end of the year send it there with a note from your child, or bring your child to present the funds. Learning to save will serve them well later in life, and the awareness of charitable giving will provide your child with a sense of empowerment; knowing that each of us can have an impact on the world with our deeds and actions.*

- *"Adopt" a cause for your family. My family foundation has organized an event for almost thirty years for Meals on Wheels an organization that feeds the homebound hungry. My boys have attended every event, and my older son delivered meals.*
- *Thanksgiving is a great day to deliver meals to the needy. Why not work in a shelter that day with your children and celebrate your day a bit later or celebrate your holiday the next day! I took*

*Tricia's eldest son, who is best friends with my younger son, for an early Thanksgiving food delivery. We went into the parks and down side streets. A friend initially organized this and I brought my truck and lots of meals. It was an eye opener for the boys when the "invisible" street people become so real to them, blessing them warmly, and thanking them profusely. The boys were noticeably moved, and the following year they asked me to do it again. They discovered first hand that we all matter, everyone has value, and we can all do something to make other peoples' lives better.*

- *If you try to do at least one random act of kindness every day, your children will follow suit. They must understand their act does not have to be directed to someone they know. They will be happier people in general and you will be as well!*

- *Motivate your children to keep a journal of their thoughts. Ask your children to write down what they like about themselves, what they wish to improve, and tell them to review that every month and they can decide on their "grade." If they want to improve in an area you have talent in, take the time or find someone who does, to help your child. There is nothing more disheartening than knowing you fall short in an area and not having the skills or tools to improve, even though the desire is there. As a parent, be aware of your child's feelings of accomplishment, but also understand their lack of competency concerns. My older son who became an advanced math student initially felt insecure in that area when younger. My younger son bemoans the fact that he is not a bigger boned kid because he wanted to continue in the football program. Each has found their personal way. My older son practiced, began to excel in a masterful way in math, and was accepted into a competitive engineering program, although he has now decided to study philosophy and is enjoying it immensely. My younger son has taken up volleyball and excels at the game and has made new friends on the team. I tell my children, "We are born in America with equal rights, but none of us are born with equal abilities in every area, and that is fine; we will each find our own pathway." My mom would say, "You need to go and find your spot in the sunshine."*

Through education and hard work, many things are possible. I do tell my children that education is their door to many life choices, but I do not insist that can be absolutely "anything" they want to be because I think it is an exaggerated and unrealistic mantra. (I did tell them when they are young, if they truly want it, go for it!) But later I was slightly more discerning with my cheerleading. Some folks would disagree with my tactics. I started to be more realistic when my children developed more critical thinking skills. I would love to sing opera, but I cannot carry a tune. I might learn to improve, but I will never be good enough to perform with the Metropolitan Opera. I am a great believer that some people are born with certain extraordinary musical, artistic, or mathematical gifts, others have different endowments, and that we all have our own unique ways of excelling and being our best in this world. We need to discover what our dominant talent, passion, and purpose is. Always encourage your child, through letters or cards filled with words or praise, a special dinner, or outing to an event they enjoy for earning a great report card. However, don't give false praise. I believe strongly in merit. Praise for effort. You can praise for hard work, even if the outcome is not as brilliant as either you or they might have hoped. However, if you praise half-hearted effort, then you merely encourage mediocre performance or laziness. Also, this past era of parents feeling that any criticism negatively affects their child's fragile self-esteem is ludicrous. I am one parent who feels it created a false image of the world. In the outside world, people are rewarded for effort, good work, and competition is fierce. We need to raise children to know that study and research, tenacity, honesty, and law-abiding behaviors are the actions that garner praise and rewards. As for those who have succeeded through ill-gotten means, I believe for many their downfall awaits. For those that continue on, I wonder how their other primary relationships function. I believe that a person who "embezzles" in his or her professional life does so in private life as well, and I feel the reciprocal holds true.

- *Teaching your children that the measurement of success is not defined by how much money they earn, but includes how happy they feel at their core, and how contented they are with their family and life choices is true success.*

- *Make family albums together, speak about your ancestors, this provides your children with a sense of continuity, even in less* intact families of which there certainly are many of these days. There is a story to be told and cherished within every family.

- Draw together (take an art class together or send you child). My son loved to bring home his creations. It solved the "what to get mom for her birthday or Mother's Day" dilemma.

- Bake and cook together, share meals, do laundry together, and give each child a chore. Young men will especially benefit from the independence they gain knowing they can feed and care for their own home. If they do marry, you will have a happier daughter-in-law.

- Create a picnic, whether outdoors or on a blanket indoors, with potted flowers arranged around the floor. You can feature a culinary creation by each child.

- From an early age, post a Responsibility Board. Chores can be both unrewarded and rewarded. Some work should be part of the family unit. Perhaps you can create other chores where the child volunteers or earns money, a trip to a movies, extra TV privileges, or computer time. Chores that do not get done should receive demerits. I believe that poor behavior should have consequences, such as loss of privileges.

- If you are a religious family, worshipping together is a wonderful time to speak about values or just share time. Perhaps go on a "pilgrimage" to a holy place.

- The economy has been difficult for many, devastating for others. Find a community center and offer to volunteer in exchange for your children's participation in an art or athletic program.

- If you have the means to help a family, financially or with your time, do so. You will find that you are enlightened and uplifted. If you can include your children in the process, it will enrich their lives enormously.

# For You, I Wish
## A Walk on the Beach

*I walked the sandy shores of the Atlantic today, in awe that no matter what fragment of an ocean you walk, what state, country, or continent, a walk next to the salty waters brings calm and serenity. I thought of you and I wondered if I am doing my job right. Your world, moving at a pace I cannot catch, filled with electronics and peer pressure. Can I compete? Can I inspire you? When you look to the horizon, do you contemplate the world beyond? Do you marvel at the sun's reflection glistening across the water? Do you think about the endless life swimming below? Stop child, let me open your mind. Scoop up a handful of sand, let it run through your fingers, mesmerizing you by its feel, become amazed in the uniqueness of a seashell washed to shore. Let me compete with your world. Watch a flock of birds soar above and question their line formation, ponder the tide coming and going and its relationship to the moon and then I will know I am doing my job right. I question, can I compete with the wonders of your world with the wonders of mine? Explore these marvels and never forget that when a stranger shares your walk, smile and say, "Hello" I recognize my job with you is plentiful, but if I can show you some of this, I know we are off to a good start. For you, I wish a walk on the beach.*

"The hardest part about showing children the wonders of the world is first spotting them ourselves."

- Tricia LaVoice

# Reflection

*The hardest part about showing children the wonders of the world is first spotting them ourselves. It is easy to get caught up in the pressures of life, the fast pace, and to lose focus in the exhaustion of it all. Nature greatly inspired my father, so I was fortunate to be raised finding wonder in my world as a child. This was one of the greatest gifts my father offered me. We would go on walks together quite often and he would always point out what amazed him, like a shadow cast by a tree, the beautiful craftsmanship of a spider web. He would ask me where I thought the sun was going as it waved goodnight to me and talked about the lightning bugs lighting the summer night's sky. He gave me a sense of wonder about my world that could never be taken away.*

*It is easy to overlook so many of Mother Nature's miracles, but when we take a moment to think about them, they are endless. I try to point them out to my children, just as my father did for me. To plant a seed in the garden is a wonderful task to share, but to first place the seed in a child's hand and express the fascination that this little seed will grow under the earth while we sleep, sprout in the spring, and bring us food or beauty makes the whole task that much more valuable for them.*

*I do not know what life will bring to my children, whether they will find love; have good fortune and good health. I can prepare them for their futures to the best of my ability and pray for the best, but I cannot control it. By opening their eyes to the miracles of life, teaching them to see and not take anything for granted, I am assured that they will always have a moon in their sky to watch wane and wax over the month and bees in their gardens to watch pollinate the flowers. Rich or poor, alone or with families of their own, the wonder of life will always be waiting for them outside their doors if they know how to see it. I make mistakes in my parenting every day and I am constantly learning about being a mom, but knowing that I am giving my children the gift of wonderment offers me comfort that they are going to be just fine.*

"Every corner of our world has a surprise to offer, it shares those gifts with all of us. We just need to look, and take the time to see, to really see what is before us. To listen, and truly hear; and to feel, and enjoy the sensations; to inhale deeply and enjoy the aroma of life. Discover your walk on the beach, your climb to a mountain top; your moment in the sun, and bask. Even in the smallest of spaces there is the mystery of nature and the power of your spirit which shares it."

-Barbara Lazaroff

# *Words and Actions from Barbara*

May you remember your journeys and lessons of life always, so that one day you can realize how many steps you have taken, how far you have climbed and how many lives you have touched. Along your way, remember as parents, one of your missions is to inspire your child's journey and teach them to be able to witness and appreciate the miracles in life. These lessons will help them emphasize how we must protect the natural magnificence of our world.

- *When on the East coast, get up early and take your child to watch the sunrise. It's especially wonderful if you can get to a beach and watch it rise over the ocean.*

- *Watch the sunset. Look for the final glow as the sun disappears and make a wish. If on the West coast, this is a beautiful experience to watch over the Pacific Ocean.*

- *Research "full moons" and watch how the moon wanes and waxes all month long.*

- *Lie on your backs together, looking up at the sky. Try to find interesting shapes in the clouds.*

- *One evening look up at the sky and find patterns in the stars. Teach your child about the various constellations. Wish.*

- *Sit and watch an army of ants at work.*

- *Watch the bees fly from one flower to the next. Talk about pollination.*

- *Just admire the fascinating patterns of a spider web.*

- *Plant sunflowers seeds together. When they grow watch how the sunflower faces move throughout the day to follow the sun.*

- *There are many breathtaking shows on television about the wonders of nature. Watch them together, point out what* captivates you. Ask your child what particularly moves them, and if they would like to learn more about that subject.

• Skip rocks down by a river or lake.

• Visit the wonders of an aquarium, a planetarium, a zoo, or a natural habitat museum. Read about the environments you are to visit with your child, (and his friends perhaps), Study a bit about some of the animals or plants prior to the trip, this will inspire your child to ask questions. Perhaps find a guide at the locations; they will be passionate and knowledgeable about their subjects. If the location is too large to cover in one day, inquire what areas are most appropriate to visit first for your child's age.

• Take a walk around the neighborhood and try to identify neighbors plants and flowers. You could take a camera, photograph the flora, and try look them up on the internet. You can make signs for your garden areas; the plant nurseries sell small identifiers to post which you can write on with waterproof ink. Have the children help make a personal botanical garden. Plant a vegetable and herb garden; this provides a time of delight; particularly as their crop comes in!

• Go snorkeling, or if you can afford it and are adventurous learn to scuba dive together. Explore caves, take nature hikes, collect specimens of and rocks, start a collection. Collect and identify flora; make a book of pressed flowers and plants. Watch out for the Poison Ivy!

• Create a more beautiful world! Organize a group of parents and children to adopt and clean up a park, or a portion of the beach; or perhaps tidy the neighborhood you live in, Plant some flowers together your street. This will give the children a sense of pride as well.

• Help out in animal shelter, a veterinarian's office, volunteer with your child at an "adopt a pet" day. Many children find enormous joy interacting with animals. These will be memorable days of providing much needed attention and care to these dear creatures. Animals provide unconditional love, and are glorious teachers."

"Study nature, love nature, stay close to nature.

It will never fail you"

– Frank Lloyd Wright, Architect


"My life is like a stroll on the beach...

as near to the edge as I can go."

– Thoreau


"To myself I am only a child playing on the beach, while vast

oceans of truth lie undiscovered before me."

- Isaac Newton

# For You, I Wish
## The Sky

*Beautiful boy hiding behind your coat of armor, the world has betrayed you and society robs your gender the right to grieve. Only the salt from your tears can melt your shield, but protect yourself now as you must. It cannot keep me from seeing your watering eyes, feeling your hurting heart. You feel vulnerable and exposed, naked in a cold world with many roads to travel, holding only a broken compass. Remember, when learning to walk, you fell again and again and I was there to pick you up, but then you fell again and you alone pulled yourself to safety. You cried from your bed and I came to soothe you, you cried again and you alone soothed yourself back to slumber. Beneath your metal coat, you possess the strength to see you through. What you don't know, my beautiful boy, is that while you were picking yourself up, I was moving furniture from your way and as you soothed yourself back to sleep, I was lying on the floor at the foot of your bed. Oceans will separate us, mountains will divide us, but I am always with you. When you wake in the morning, look to the sun and let it warm your face, knowing I am looking to the same sun. In the early evening, look to the stars and wish, knowing I am wishing on the same stars. And most of all, my beautiful boy, look to the sky and know my love for you. There is no beginning, no end, no start, no finish; my love is everywhere, behind you, in front of you, to the sides of you. I wish you the sky of my love, grand and infinite, always and forever.*

"There is no beginning, no end, no start, no finish;

my love is everywhere."

- Tricia LaVoice

# Reflection

*I recently read a statistic that one in four or five women, I can't remember exactly, would rather be a man than a woman. Thinking about this option, I concluded for myself that no matter how easy it makes camping or getting ready to go out at night, no matter what the benefits in the work place are, I could not imagine living a life where my emotions could not run free.*

*This winter, my family and I watched a lot of the Olympics together, and I must have gotten teary ten times over the two week period. I cried watching the parents swell up over their children's victories, I cried with the athlete who won and lost, and as most observers, I cried watching the ice skater compete only two days after her mother passed away – not to mention the tears I shed while watching the horrific story on the bobsledder who had a fatal accident during practice the day before the events began. My children really did not even pay attention to me and my tears. I love to be free to not only watch the athletes, but to be emotionally engaged, to experience a taste of the passion they must all be feeling. I am not sure how it would have gone over if it were one of my sons or my husband who showed this much emotion during the games. I suspect we all may have been alarmed. Does this mean males feel any less? Have we conditioned them to be less sensitive?*

*Recently, we had a couple visiting us who had twin five-year-olds, a boy and a girl. The couple started parenting late in life, and although they get physically exhausted easily, they have the advantage of parenting with more life experiences than the rest of us. At one time during their visit, the little boy fell and hurt himself, but not too badly. He ran to his father, who picked him up and held him, and he whispered to him, "Go ahead and cry, let it out." I loved seeing the sensitivity shared between father and son, when I had expected to hear him say, "You're okay," which I would have thought was the appropriate response before I heard the more sensitive one given.*

*It is easy to get a five-year-old who has been raised to express his emotions to communicate his feelings, but by the time our boys are young men, a shield goes up for many, making it hard to reach them. These bottled-up feelings usually have a tendency to manifest themselves in ugly ways,* which is no good for anyone. Although our sons will act like they do not want to talk to us, which they probably do not, it is very important that we speak our love to them. They must understand that we are there standing still and available at any given moment if they need us. When they pretend their hearts are not hurting, we must speak of a hurting heart and validate the emotion that we know they are suppressing. They will tell us to go away and shut doors, but they will hear us. When we are fortunate enough to get them to open up to us, we must be very careful with the words we choose, for the shield is quick to go back up.

Boys are so wonderful and loving, and when raised with sensitivities, grow to be fabulous husbands and fathers themselves. Love them and talk to them, for shields of armor may provide refuge, but they are not sound proof.

# *Words and Actions from Barbara*

Dr. Seuss proclaimed, "A person's a person, no matter how small." Therefore, I believe that a betrayal, a disappointment, a family relocation, a broken heart, the death of a beloved pet, or the profound loss of a loved one, can feel as painful to a small person, or a young adult, as to an adult. We often believe that our children will heal because they have youth and the passage of time on their side. Often that is very true, and in many cases the slights and failures they experience are not life altering and will often be forgotten in the broader landscape of their lives. However, there a certain rainstorms that may blacken their psyches, "their skies" for years to come.

Tricia wrote this Wish for one of my sons at a particularly difficult juncture in his life. His heart had been broken and he had come to realize that a person he had trusted with his innermost feelings was disloyal. It was a moment I could relate to, but of course this was his pain, his moment, his loss. My job as a mother was to try to support him as best I could, and this varied depending on the day of the week, the time of day, and his point in the healing process. I was on call, occasionally it was exhausting, and however his trust in my love for him became an opportunity to bond.

- *Try to speak with your children every day about what is going on in their lives; ask about school, interests. They likely will not offer as much information as they get older, but at least they know you care. When they are at the non-communicative stage in their development be patient, be understanding, try to restrain yourself from being overbearing with your concern. Let them know you are always open to hearing them. Your teenage children may be critical, feel you are as well; they will only truly know what it feels like to be a concerned parent when they have their own children; I have therefore stopped trying to explain myself!*

- *Do not be intimated to discuss drugs, alcohol, sex and other issues that may be uncomfortable not only for your child, but you as well. Start communications when they are young so they are comfortable discussing these topic. I started talking to my boys early in their development, delicately at first and with greater detail as they got older.*

- *Learn to communicate on their terms. One of my sons does not answer his cell or respond to his email too often; when he lost his computer it then made emails impossible! He did text however, so I took up his form of communication, and taught my mom how to text as well so she could "talk" to him at college.*

- *Send care packages of their favorite cookies, a hand knit cap or scarf, amusing cards, a little fun money, a recent family photo from home of their pet or sibling.*

- *If you are deeply concerned about your child's well being call her closest friends to check up, express your concerns, they may offer you some suggestions.*

- *If your child is away or living on their own, let them know they have a ticket and a place at home anytime they need the comfort and safety of their family.*

- *When our children are small we can play games such as, "What was the best moment of your day, what was your worst?" It is amazing what they will share and what you will learn about their concerns, fears, and hopes. Remember keeping communication flowing requires consistent exchanges of ideas with an open mind, this needs to start very early.*

- *Ask them to draw a picture of the best day of the week, and describe it, you do this as well. This is particularly effective with younger children.*

- *Relate some stories from your own childhood about embarrassing moments, disappointments, things that frightened you, moments of failure and times of achievement. My mom told me some of the funniest stories and I have since asked her to tell my children. One truly memorable anecdote in particular was about a strict chorus teacher who was horrid to her and the other children. The teacher* was only concerned about making a good impression on the parents. When the day of the big auditorium performance arrived she would not let one of the boys go to the bathroom, as the chorus began to sing he could not restrain himself any longer, he started to relieve himself and thirty other children followed on stage! This story always made me feel better no matter what embarrassing moment I experienced as a child!

• It is extremely important for you to get professional advice for your child if you suspect a serious emotional or physical problem. If you are confused about whether or not some issue is merely an age appropriate behavior, or a signpost of a possible underlying illness, ask friends, family members and consult with counselors, about what they see and feel about your child's behavioral patterns or responses in certain situations. However, as the mother you are usually the best judge of your child's needs. There are those instances where parents are in denial, a father who would not believe his son was autistic, a mother I know who could not admit to herself that her pre-teen son was smoking, and another whose son was using her prescription drugs. The sooner you deal with a problem, the sooner you can make progress towards raising a healthy, productive child.

• Help your child develop a strong E.Q., (emotional quotient or emotional I.Q.). We spend an enormous amount of time and finances on the intellectual development of our children, but studies now reveal that a person's E.Q. may be as important, if not more vital, to the overall success of individuals developing healthy personal and professional relationships and dynamics. There are many books and online informational studies and videos about the importance of E.Q.; as well as, seminars and tutorials on how to train our children, and ourselves, in expanding these skills. Self-awareness, self-management, social awareness, and relationship management all require learning both verbal and non-verbal cues, conflict resolution, stress reduction, controlling impulsive feelings and behaviors; all necessary tools and skills for survival in order to live long and well.

• *Support your children, be a cheerleader, and a nurturer, but if you truly want the best for them you will not minimize your responsibility of disciplining them. You may be looking at the same sky, but remember to remind them if they want to fly straight and strong and arrive at their destinations, they must open their hearts, keep their minds and bodies healthy, cast off their protective masks, live life bravely and fully. They know you will always be on their team; however it will ultimately be their own strengths, independence and choices that will be the defining factors in where they land.*

"Each friend represents a world in us,

a world possibly not born until they arrive, and it is

only by this meeting that a new world is born."

- Anais Nin, Author

# For You, I Wish

## Your Bloom

*My child, you are a bud in bloom but growing so fast, I yearn to slow the rain and sun that encourages you. Soon you will be a beautiful flower off dazzling the world far from my view. Never forget that you are my rose; if you sit on the table or rest in the garden, if basking in the moonlight or lazing in the sunshine, you are my rose. Move forward with your elegance, but remain alert; life is not always a bed of roses. There will be times when the wind and rain knock your petals to the ground; stay strong, you cannot be defeated if you are creating potpourri. Your sister roses will come in shapes and colors special for them; respect their differences and rejoice in the array of splendor you create together. Let your beauty grace the eye, let your fragrance perfume the air, but take care not to wound with your thorns. Life may not always be a bed of roses, but life is beautiful and you, my child, are always my rose. For you, I wish your bloom.*

It has been said: "Use what talents you possess:
the woods would be very silent if no birds sang there
except those that sang best."

- Henry Van Dyke, Author

# Reflection

*The relationship shared between mother and daughter will be the most influential relationship of a daughter's life. Letting a daughter know she is loved by her mother unconditionally is essential for her to be able to love herself and love others, while having the self-esteem she will need to thrive in today's world. As she becomes a wife, mother, and friend to others, the love she received and continues to receive from her own mother will give her the strength, courage, and wisdom she needs to succeed in these relationships. And yet, there are many other lessons that must be taught, and although she will listen to what her mother says, mostly she will copy what her mother does. Telling her that gossip is not nice will have little effect on her if she hears her mother gossiping. Verbally emphasizing the importance of education to her is wonderful, but seeing her mother read a book is more effective. She needs to see her mother's compassion, feel her mother's confidence, and witness her mother's self-respect so that she, in turn, will have it for herself.*

*I love, love, love raising a daughter, although I admit that it scares me. I want to protect her from the world, yet I know I cannot. I would never sleep another wink if I allowed myself to think about all the possible dangers to a young girl, so I try to simply trust that she is okay and will be okay. Some may consider me neurotic, but I just consider myself a mother.*

*Being creative and having fun while teaching our daughters life lessons can be good for everyone. One of my favorite books is "The Red Tent" by Anita Diamant, which tells the story of women in biblical times. What fascinates me most about the women in this book is the glorious celebration they hold for young girls when they begin to menstruate, marking their ability to give birth. After proper ritual, the girls are honored into the tent with the other women where they gather once a month and to give birth.*

*I thought of all the events and birthdays I celebrated with my daughter and questioned why this amazing milestone should slip through the cracks without tribute. I also hoped that by celebrating her first menstrual cycle, it would not only stress the gift of childbearing, but also the responsibility that went along with this power.*

*My friends were on alert, and we waited for Olivia's period to come. When it finally did, she was a sport and only slightly resisted the attention, and allowed my wonderful friend Carlene to host a "Red Tent" party. All my girlfriends joined in the fun and dressed up in flowing gauze dresses, bringing presents to share in this welcoming of Olivia into womanhood. I rented two beautiful Moroccan tents, which we set up in Carlene's yard overlooking the Los Angeles skyline. We kept Olivia and her five friends in the smaller tent while about twenty-five of us women prepared the party in the larger tent. As the sun set, we gathered outside the girls' tent and took turns sharing words of wisdom with them. Then we all returned to the larger tent and celebrated the night away with good food and song.*

*I am not sure if the celebration influenced Olivia's perception, but I do know we had a ton of fun and it was important to me to recognize this significant occasion in her life. Raising a daughter comes with many challenges - but how amazing it is to watch a flower in bloom.*

"To the buds, when you bloom, you will be the women

who will educate the next generation of girls and boys;

you will make global policy, grow food, find cures, create art,

music and dance, and hopefully end wars. Learn, grow,

blossom and give back. Leave a forest of love and

knowledge behind you."

- Barbara Lazaroff

# *Words and Actions from Barbara*

I always tell my girlfriends and their daughters to be prepared for their lives, (I learned that as a Brownie). Instruct your daughters to study, listen well, observe carefully, travel, and seek out mentors. So often in the past, and even presently, young women are defined in terms of their external beauty. There is nothing as enduring as internal loveliness and strength gathered from education, experience, and enlightenment. Certainly, we want our young women to better themselves professionally through professional networking organizations, or getting a degree or advanced degree; however there is also much personal benefit to be achieved through helping others through charity. One of my favorite proverbs is, "A bit of fragrance always clings to the hand that gives you roses." If women hope to produce a world of strong proficient sisterhood, education is the first step to a better life, and team work is the other. I have often said, "We are a sisterhood. One woman's success is every woman's success, and we are all strengthened when we extend our hands and help another young woman along the path."

- *It is essential to have credit in your own name. Tell your friends to do the same, even if they are married.*

- *Be prepared as best you can, emotionally and educationally, to be able to provide for yourself and your children in the future. If you develop well honed intellectual and personal skills and tools, you can survive the loss of a job, divorce and will be flexible and resilient enough to refocus and pursue a new life path.*

- *Always remember, too, that you are blessed in life. We all go through tough times; remarkably some of the struggles in our lives turn into opportunities. Be grateful for the gifts you do have; keeping a positive attitude attracts greater possibilities.*

- *You must exert energy and work moment by moment to fashion your own destiny. Be confident in your abilities, but continue to work diligently on improving your weaknesses.*

# For You, I Wish
## Your Way

*I anger you; you flail your arms, gulp water as you struggle to stay afloat. You see me standing on the ocean's edge, holding the life preserver that has saved you so many times before. I watch the current pull you farther from safety. You reach your arms to me, but I remain still. You must move now, I can no longer hold you up, so hold my words close. Remain alert, the waters can change at any time. Swim with the current as much as possible and let its energy move you. When it gets choppy, swim harder; when you are too tired to swim another stroke, swim your hardest. When you hit a riptide, stay calm. Watch out for sharks and barracudas. Your heart pounds and you tread water, not moving from your place. But rest assured the ocean is grand and full of beauty. It can take you around the world and back. The salt of its waters will heal your wounds and the fish from its core will nourish your body. If you trust and relax, you will float much of your journey, you will see an array of beauty in color and form. Remember to swim like the dolphins jumping through the air, glide like a sea turtle, dream like a mermaid. Over the years, spend time in a school of fish, swim solo like a beluga whale. You see me standing on the water's edge holding a life preserver and you are confused as to why I do not toss it your way. Know my arms tremble in resistance. You are frightened and so am I. I yearn to swallow the seven seas so you can walk to safety; I yearn to battle every creature known to the ocean's water. I must let you go now and wish you your way, but of all my words, hold these words closest: I stand apart from you now, watching from the ocean's edge, but I am prepared, and if you lose your way, I will swim around the globe in hunt for you. This I promise.*

"One day it became clear that they were their own persons,

these were their lives, their journeys."

- Patricia LaVoice

# Reflection

*I am not sure how many of us really know what parenting is all about when we first decide to start a family. I, for one, did not. I remember wanting sweet little babies that I could hold and play with and dress in cute clothes. They were MY babies, MY children, and then one day it became clear that they were their own persons, these were their lives, their journeys. The thought was actually overwhelming for me. It is one thing to make mistakes with MY children, but making mistakes with someone else's life is a whole other story. One day you're concerned with getting them into a good preschool and having them use good manners so everyone sees that YOUR children are well-behaved, and then the next, you suddenly realize that they feel emotional pain, they fear, they experience self-doubt. The responsibility is huge: making sure they grow up liking themselves, capable of handling hardships while having limited anxieties. And then, there is love and our never-ending influence on how they will perceive it, accept it, and bestow it.*

*Preparing our children to become adults takes hard work, trust, and courage. Chances are, they will encounter heartbreaks, difficult bosses, and callous coworkers throughout their lives and we will not be there to fight their battles and protect them. It is our responsibility to love them, prepare them, and let them live their own lives. Our greatest challenge is in discovering just how to do that.*

*By letting them make mistakes and experience emotional pain, our children learn the lessons in life that give them the self-confidence, self-assurance, and self-esteem we want them to have as adults. I like to look at universal conditions as nature's way of telling me when to pay attention. If my child was the only child experiencing hardships and dealing with playground politics, I would worry much more. However, when I see all the children experiencing similar trials and tribulations, I believe it is nature's way of letting them practice before adulthood.*

*This did not always come so easy to me. I remember the first time Olivia came home from kindergarten crying about another child. I was just about to call the bully's mother when my sister called me and talked me down. Luckily for me, my sisters and Rich's sisters all have older kids, so I get to benefit from their experiences when I am open to listening. My sister explained that this was just the beginning of the drama with friends that my daughter would bring home over the years, and I should remember that there are always two sides to every story. I certainly could not be getting involved and calling mothers all my life, so it would be much better to guide her in handling her own battles. I learned to get involved only when my intervention is truly needed, and to let my children take responsibility for and control of their personal lives.*

*Preparing our children for adulthood is by no means easy — but it is crucial. I would have had a dozen kids if all I had to do was love them like I did when they were babies. Holding them is easy; letting them go is the difficult part.*

"You can be the glorious dandelion on the winds of time that sends out messages of hope, creating change, making your dreams come true and enlightening those around you."

- Barbara Lazaroff

# *Words and Actions from Barbara*

So many people in our culture judge success in terms of the clothes you have on your back, what kind of car you're driving, or where you live. I enjoy beautiful things and I do collect, but only later in life do you realize these things don't necessarily bring you happiness. What I want my boys to remember...

- *Never forget your family responsibilities and to honor yourself as well. These are your first priorities.*

- *Working for success in every aspect of life is something you will always have to do. Professional success can be fleeting if you are not on top of your work and the changing technologies and zeitgeist. Remember, if you measure success in terms of financial gains or status alone, to the exclusion of family and friendship you may be disappointed to find your life less fulfilling than you imagined.*

- *Some people believe if marriage or friendship is work, it isn't worth it. Untrue; all relationships require reviews and adjustments.*

- *We change, life changes, and to stay together, you have to be committed to communication, compromise and sustaining the family unit, your friendships and your professional relationships. However, if we are not cherished, respected or appreciated we must know when to move on.*

- *Surround yourself with do-ers with purpose and heart; learn from them, participate, add value and they will guide you. Shrug off the users, the manipulators and naysayers.*

- *Stand up straight – your emotional and physical "posture" affects everything. Attitude has more to do with your day than the actual events of the day. How you respond to your environment changes it; change it for the better, no matter what comes your way.*

- *Think and act responsibly; what you say and do affects so many, and these individuals, in turn, affects others. Excess in alcohol or food, lack of sleep, and other personal abuses, does not bode well for your prime performance and negatively affects others.*

# For You, I Wish
## Your Place Amongst Women

*I was born a child to the clan, a pack animal, a social creature. Always at my mother's side until the day she whispered, "Go child, sit with your sisters by the fire. Find your place amongst women." There I formed my thoughts, my values, my way. I found safety, purpose, love. As we grew tall, we laughed together, ventured beyond our camps, shared visions and dreams. As we grew taller, we stood at each others' sides as we wed and birthed. The children played as the men went off to hunt. My sisters shadowed my children, fed my husband as I theirs. Kindred spirits, we worked together to nurture our people. Then one morning, I awoke to find myself missing. My first family and I separated from our kin. We walked the woods alone. Soon the children went off to play and my mate to hunt. Lost without my sisters, I cried my eyes blue. Defined by their words, dependent on their guidance, I stumbled in their absence. Was I too reliant? Maybe. Left with no choice, I picked myself up alone. I gained a self respect, a wisdom that only could be found in my loneliness. Yet, for every one step I took in self pride, I took two in missing them; for every one step I took in newfound insight, I took two in wishing time backwards. Isolation became part of my journey with much to offer, yet I did not need it to remind me that I was born a child of the clan, a pack animal, a social creature. I now whisper to daughters of all clans, "Go child, sit with your sisters by the fire. Find your place amongst women. Trust her and earn her trust, you will see clearer and find your feet planted to the ground for this: love her and let her love you, you will be a better mother and wife for this; care for her and she will, in return, care for you. When in her presence, put away all jealousies, competitions, and betrayals. You may choose to walk alone, but see through my eyes, when you walk with your sisters, the journey is simpler and so much sweeter." It is never too soon or too late to find your place amongst women. For you, I wish you your place amongst women.*

"It is never too soon or too late to find

your place amongst women "

- Tricia LaVoice

# Reflection

*It wasn't long after we moved to Connecticut when I was standing in line at a coffee shop, waiting my turn, and overheard a conversation between two young girls. They looked like they were about thirteen or fourteen years old, and from the look of their outfits, had just come from riding lessons. There was no effort to eavesdrop on my part, for they spoke loudly and clearly as if proud of what they were saying. Their conversation gained momentum and vengeance as they gossiped away about another girl at the barn. They criticized her riding abilities, her outfits, and even her horse. I was glad when I saw the mother turn to them, hoping she would put an end to the noise pollution, but I was shocked when she joined in and began gossiping herself. There was no talk on tolerance, forgiveness, compassion, or the evils of judgment.*

*Growing up with girlfriends and having girlfriends as an adult woman is a priceless gift. But a friendship is a relationship and, like all relationships, they take time and effort. You have to have each others' backs. You have to have love, loyalty, respect, trust, and acceptance. You must be able to forgive and work through the fights, no matter how petty or serious, if you hope to maintain true, deep friendships. Teaching our daughters the importance of being a good friend and having good friends will offer them a lifetime of support and love.*

*But women will play other roles in our daughters' lives, and it is important that our daughters know how to get along with them. They may have sisters-in-law, mothers-in-law; they will most likely have female co-workers and maybe a female boss. Female mentors are huge. I started collecting them when I was young, with my big sister being my first, and now have an array of women mentors who have taught me more about life than all my college courses combined.*

*Learning how to get along with other women comes very easily for some and is more challenging for others. However, all women benefit from having female friends – friends you want to sit up with all night long and talk to, friends to hold your secrets, to tell you not to worry, and friends to cry to when life gets too hard. Our girlfriends are our rocks when we are unsteady, our light when things are dark. Having girlfriends is a trea-*

*sure, and we must stress to our daughters the importance of having these friendships throughout their lives. The best way to ensure this is to begin by teaching our daughters how to be good girlfriends themselves. The best way to teach them this concept is letting them watch us being our genuine selves.*

"Go child, sit with your sisters by the fire.

Find your place amongst women."

- Tricia LaVoice

# *Words and Actions from Barbara*

Ambition rocks, treachery does not! Other women are your sisters. Treat them with respect - with the same respect you would like to receive. Don't underestimate a less experienced sister; you may be working for her one day! Ways to join the sisterhood:

- *Explore a professional association or social networking group pertaining to your career and interests. Join up and participate!*

- *Connect with organizations that are already a part of your life. For example, if you have children, try joining the PTA, or become a leader for a Girl Scout troop.*

- *Volunteer at a local hospital, reading to young children or the elderly; bring your daughter along, it will positively influence her future behavior.*

- *Instructing a young girl how to swim, knit, use a computer, bake, ride a bike, open a savings account, or properly organize a research paper, is an immense gift of self-confidence that will affect the rest of her life.*

- *On the fun side of meeting sisters, join a book club or dare to start one.*

- *If you are the athletic type, join a tennis tournament, take up yoga, or go away on a hiking retreat.*

- *Look for walk-a-thons in your area or volunteering opportunities in your area and meet great women while helping others.*

- *Start a professional organization; I founded a group with seven other women nearly 17 years ago, and there are thousands of members now; supporting a terrific networking system, continuing education and scholarship programs.*

- *Serve on a non-profit board, or a committee. Or if you are asked and feel equipped and can afford the time, serve on corporate board. You will meet other accomplished women, with similar or differing interests; network for business, as well as friendship.*

Learn how to recognize the manipulator, or the home or job wrecker. Do not get intimate with women that step on anyone to "get ahead"; if they can do it to another woman in business, or have relations with a married man, lie to their colleagues, take credit for other peoples' work, or are abusive to assistants and people in positions of service; Beware! If they have no conscience about being deceitful with others, they may betray you next. Befriend women of integrity; don't be impressed by the glamour or status of a woman if there is no underlying substance.

"Be a genuine sister, mother, friend: find your place amongst women - It is indeed a noble place to be."

- Barbara Lazaroff

"There is a special place in hell for women

who do not help other women."

- Madeleine K. Albright,

Former U.S. Ambassador to the United Nations,
and former Secretary of State

# For You, I Wish
## A Season of Love

*If I could write you spring, I would compose a rainbow and stretch it near and far for you to climb and witness the Seven Wonders of the World. If I could write you summer, I would compose a rushing river and float you to the sea where you could sing with the mermaids and ride the backs of sea-horses. If I could write you autumn, I would compose you into an artist so your brush could glide across a colorful landscape creating a new earth. If I could write your winter, I would compose you a snowflake to float you way above the clouds so you could soar throughout the stars. But I do not know how to write you spring and summer or winter and fall. I cannot compose rainbows and rivers or snowflakes and artists. All I know is how to write you love, to compose for you the words of my heart, the whispers of my dreams, to hold your hand in mine, and love you. For you, I wish you a season of love.*

"I must trust the world to be kind to my children,

and when it is not, I will be there waiting with open arms."

– Tricia LaVoice

# Reflection

*If only we held magic in our hands to grant their dreams and protect them from harm. But life does not work that way. I remember being so prepared for the birth of our first child, Olivia. I read all the right books, attended the seminars, and had plenty of experience babysitting growing up. I was playing with dolls from the moment I could hold one and now I was getting a real one. I could not stand waiting another minute to kiss her, smell her, and hold her close. I was more prepared to become a mother than anything I had ever done in my life until the reality check hit me like a ton of bricks. I think it was around day five. We were home from the hospital and my mother had returned to her house, leaving Rich and me in charge. I believe it was her runny nose that had us calling the ER at three in the morning. We were unaware of the vulnerability that came with parenting. There was no way to plan for it. Ten months earlier she was a thought, now she was our entire world. No one can prepare you for the love you will feel, or the fear that goes along with that love.*

*Now, when I read this Wish, I yearn more than ever to be able to grant them their dreams and more importantly protect them. About a year ago our youngest son, Bobby, was clearing his throat a lot and shrugging his shoulders. I was emailing Leeza trying to describe his symptoms as if they were similar to someone with Tourettes. Double checking my spelling, I googled Tourettes and began reading; onset between the ages of seven and nine, most common in boys, symptoms include clearing of the throat and shrugging of the shoulders. Bobby was eight at the time. Panic rushed through my body as I frantically typed to Leeza, freaking out. She tried to calm me saying this was just a neurological hiccup and not to worry. But I sat up until four in the morning talking to my sister in law, Dorothy, drowning myself in wine. It took weeks to get an appointment with the best neurologist in town. Barbara flew out and went with Rich and me to the appointment. The doctor was very laid back and explained that Bobby most likely had Tourettes and that the next two years would be most telling. Over the last year, Bobby's symptoms waned and waxed. Every time I thought it was a growing pain and behind us, he would start a new tic. As I write this, he is in a phase where he makes little sounds all the time, sweet sounds. I listen to him playing with friends—laughing and having a blast—but all I hear are the sounds in between. I catch myself being angry at silly things and losing my patience with those around me as I accept that Bobby may always have Tourettes. How can I protect him? How can I make his world okay? Then I rethink it and I see Bobby is fine. He does not have a childhood illness that threatens his life, nor is he pain. He is not even bothered by his tics. When I ask him about his tics and if they bother him, he replies, "No, it feels good, but I know it bothers you." He is right. It does bother me, but only because I cannot protect him.*

*When reading this Wish, I find myself wishing I could paint him a perfect world to grow up in, where there is no teasing or syndromes. I want to write him a rainbow and let him swim with the mermaids; but I cannot, just like I could not stop Olivia's nose from running when she was five days old. I can try to protect them from the outside world and even themselves at times; but many things are outside a mother's control. What is in my control is my ability to love my children and hold their hands in mine. Now, I must trust the world to be kind to my children and when it's not, I will be there waiting with open arms. What more can a mother do?*

"I find myself wishing I could paint him a

perfect world to grow up in...

...many things are outside a mother's control.

What is in my control is my ability to love my

children and hold their hands in mine."

- Tricia LaVoice

"A mother  is a safe haven, a teacher of

good values and principles, a nurturer.

A mother is a disciplinarian; a mother does

whatever she has to do for her child.

A mother gives unconditional and endless love."

- Ellie Lazaroff, Barbara's mother

# *Words and Actions from Barbara*

"The grass is greener where the grass is watered." Keep reminding those you cherish that they are worthy of love, that you admire them, treasure them and you are blessed to have them in your life.

- *Avoid making judgments around your children. The less harshly they judge their world, the less they will see their world judging them.*

- *Read books on building children's self esteem.*

- *Teach them skills to become self-reliant: like cooking, sewing, changing tires on cars, welding, carpentry, plumbing; let them help you with projects, even when it might slow you down.*

- *The world can be tough, keep the home a safe place where they trust they can find love and acceptance. Have zero tolerance for sibling name calling and bullying of one another.*

- *Think of creative ways to spend time with your children. Our lives are hectic but we can turn everyday routines into fun loving memories for them simply by naming everyday situations. Call breakfast your morning "tea party." Place their orange juice in a tea cup so they feel as if they are drinking tea with you before rushing out the door. Get the mail together and try to guess how many letters and bills will be in the box and from whom. While in the car together listen to the radio and compose new lyrics to an old song.*

"Whatever they grow up to be, they are still our children, and the one most important of all things we can give to them is unconditional love. Not a love that depends on anything at all except that they are our children."

– Rosaleen Dickson, Author

# For You, I Wish
## To Say, "I Am Sorry"

*I collected all my wishes and packed them safely with my favorite blanket. I had waited anxiously for this August night's sky when stars would shoot across the galaxy showering the dark with light, showering me with wonder. Night fell, but the sky I walked below was absent of dazzle, absent of awe where I could rest my dreams. Unanticipated fog clogged the airways foiling my hopes of seeing anything tonight but the gray. I awoke to a similar morning sky and spent most of the day inside avoiding her gloom. Come dusk, I ventured to walk in her gray willing to at least enjoy the temperature she offered. Within moments of my journey her clouds parted, her fog lifted, and the sun broke through streaking my face in warmth. The light graced the surrounding foliage giving birth to an array of imaginable greens. But she did not stop there, she continued decorating her crystal blue landscape in shades of pink and orange, tranquilizing me with her beauty as if she were trying to make up for the gray she smothered me in the night before... First, I cast my eyes to the ground in remorse. Then, I lift them to meet yours in truth. I place one hand on my heart to open my soul and reach the other to you in loyalty. My words are few, but I speak in sorrow and ask for your forgiveness. For you, I wish to say, "I am sorry."*

"Saying "I am sorry" is beautiful, cleansing, and healthy. "

– Tricia LaVoice

## Reflection

*It may seem unusual to have an "I am sorry" wish in a book about mothering, but saying "I am sorry" is a big part of being a mother and a daughter. Teaching our children how to say "I am sorry" is very important if we wish them to have long-term committed relationships in their lives. Today has just begun and I know that my son Jack is expecting me to watch a movie with him tonight. However, I forgot that I must bring his brother to basketball. He will be unhappy, even with my apology, but hopefully he will feel my sorrow and understand I simply cannot be in two places at one time.*

*I never gave much thought to teaching "I am sorry" until a few years back when we had a young girl living with us who struggled with it. We worked on this for over a year before she would take responsibility and apologize when it was necessary. I wondered if she grew up having it said to her. Maybe her parents did not make the mistakes I find myself making, but I find a reason to say "I am sorry" everyday to at least one of the kids.*

*There is a lot attached to saying "I am sorry." A sincere apology must be heartfelt and genuine. You cannot worry about protecting your ego when asking for forgiveness. You must allow yourself to be wrong, and not concern yourself with the other person's role in the argument. Saying "I am sorry" is not always easy but always important for relationships to have trust and the ability grow. I have worked hard to say "I am sorry" without attaching any blame or "buts." I consider myself good at saying "I am sorry," and I think most of my loved ones would agree except my husband, Rich. He thinks I stink at it. I am still trying to figure that one out. I tease with him that maybe it is because I am always right in the marriage—he does not find that funny. I assume my ego gets in the way with my husband. I know I must continue to work on this, not only for my marriage's sake, but for my children's sake as well.*

*Saying "I am sorry" is beautiful, cleansing, and healthy. Helping our children understand the importance of this is a gift they will use all their lives. To be vulnerable, self-reflecting, and accepting of your mistakes is part of self-growth that children will need as healthy adults. Saying "I am sorry," like finding forgiveness, is a big part of loving someone. We need to say it and we need to hear it. Children need to understand that moms and dads make mistakes. When we do make mistakes and we ask forgiveness, they need to grant us that forgiveness and, when deserving, they need to learn to say "I am sorry" as well.*

"I place one hand on my heart to open my soul and reach the other to you in loyalty. My words are few, but I speak in sorrow and ask for your forgiveness."

- Tricia LaVoice

"If over time you know that the issue lies with the other person's inability to forgive; forgive yourself and move on."

- Barbara Lazaroff

# *Words and Actions from Barbara*

The ability to articulate "I am sorry" is difficult for so many; to apologize out loud directly and genuinely to another person requires courage and humility. It is a phrase we need to teach our children and one they must hear us speak to them and others. When we have engaged in discord with a spouse, a co-worker, a friend, a relative, our child or our parents, we must separate from our ego, our inflated pride, and our platform of feeling justified. If we want to maintain harmony there are times we must compromise, or simply open our hearts and arms and say this disagreement is not as important as our relationship. However, there are those moments when the wrong is so grievous that the "sorry" becomes a process. Infidelity, physical abuse, stealing, repetitive irresponsibility, continual neglect or disrespect, requires more than the obligatory, "I am sorry." Then unswerving actions will be required to elicit trust in the words, "I am sorry," and give them authentic meaning once again.

- *Learn to say "I am sorry," and promise to follow up with behavior that demonstrates you mean the words you offer up as an olive branch. I have learned one hard lesson, if there is a person in your life that says they are sorry repeatedly, but never follows through, you may have to expect less from them, or consider them toxic to your well-being and close communication.*

- *When saying you are sorry do not qualify it with a "but" or "and" or a "furthermore." Just say you are sorry and be true.*

- *If one "I am sorry" does not start the healing process, write a letter, send a card, or make a personal gift; sew it, knit it, bake it, include a note. It can just be a simple message saying you value the other person, miss them, love them, show your genuine concern and admiration; acknowledge that you understand how you hurt them by either letting them down, or criticizing them, or forgetting to show up for a luncheon date, or whatever the issue might be. If over time you know that the issue lies with the other person's inability to forgive; forgive yourself and move on.*

# For You, I Wish

## The Dignity of Jeepers

*They call her Jeepers, a name she inherited some sixty years ago. When I entered her room, I was moved by emotion, words could not prepare me for her disturbing condition as she slumped uncomfortably in her chair. Feeling uncomfortable in my own skin, I spoke quietly to her, but her vacant stare offered no response. I traveled far to be in her presence, inspired by her story. It had been many years since the thief we call Alzheimer's crept into her life, robbing her of everything, only leaving the physical to endure endless suffering, leaving no hope, no cure, devastating those who loved her so dearly. Here she breathed, living in misery, stripped of her dignity yet no one I had met before her was more deserving of self-respect or the respect of others. She had witnessed the vicious crimes of her disease in her own mother before her. She was aware that a stranger would enter her mind, diminishing her grace before she would vanish altogether into her own silence. She was fully aware of it all, yet she asked her family, for the sake of finding a cure, preventing the suffering in others, to tell her story. Footage of her demise has been witnessed by countless people, awakening the need for change; her selfless courage to make a difference has done just that, made a difference. Her caretakers moved her to the bed and she immediately curled into a fetal position as if desperately trying to return to a place of warmth and safety. I moved to the bed with her and curled at her feet and over time a peace, a comfort lying with her overtook me. There I read to her, I rubbed her aching body, and sung her a lullaby. In those moments I fell in love with this great woman, honored by the opportunity to show my gratitude. For you, I wish the dignity of Jeepers.*

"Still, there were "kisses from the angels," moments

when Mom would look right in my eyes and squeeze

my hand as if to say, "I'm here darling."

- Leeza Gibbons

# Reflection

*When living in Los Angeles, our children attended a private school in West Hollywood where I met Barbara and Leeza. I had seen Leeza on television many times in the past and it would be unfair not to admit that I was a little nervous when talking to her. However, when I learned that her mother was not well, I forgot about all those awkward feelings and spoke to her as I would speak to any woman in the face of losing her mother. We talked a lot about the pain I had experienced with the loss of my mom and what it was like for her having her mother so ill. As with Barbara, I felt our mothers brought us together and I really wanted to meet Leeza's mom. After I spoke to Leeza about it, I went home and talked it over with my husband. He supported the idea, so within two weeks I flew from Connecticut down to South Carolina, rented a car, and headed to the nursing home to meet Jeepers. I will always remember the special time I spent with her and I am very thankful for the support from those who encouraged me to take the opportunity. Leeza's mother passed away ten days after my visit. It is only appropriate that Leeza take over from here and write the reflection to this Wish. Love, Tricia.*

It was bewildering at its best, and unbearable most of the time. The questions that ran through my thoughts about my mother as she faded, memory by memory, from our grasp would often take on an echo which made the pain of the ponder even worse.

What is she thinking? Is she in pain? Is she afraid? Did she feel embarrassed, humiliated, angry? Is "she" still in there? When my Dad, my siblings, and our children would speak with her, we tried to seem normal and carry on the relationship we had always enjoyed with her. But without her easy laugh and the quick hug, there was no surface for our words to bounce off and we fell into that stilted, forced "fake" kind of banter that only served to make us feel as embarrassed as we assumed she was.

Still, there were "kisses from the angels," moments when Mom would look right in my eyes and squeeze my hand as if to say, "I'm here darling." It was after those moments that I would again be haunted by the question, "Is she locked up inside of her tangled brain, still the same strong southern steel magnolia the kids called JG, short for Jean Gibbons?"

Mom always wanted to have grandkids, but never wanted to be called Grand mom or any version of that! Even those who didn't know her well knew that she was once a powerful voice of independence and someone who presented an almost impossible balance between vulnerability and strength. Those were the qualities that prompted her to show up for her life in ways that were counter to others of her generation. Those were the qualities that stirred her resolve and prompted her to ask me to "tell her story and make it count."

She was forgetting, but she did not want to be forgotten. I used her inspiration and her spirit to create our nonprofit organization, The Leeza Gibbons Memory Foundation, and our signature program, Leeza's Place. It's what our family wished we had during our struggle: a supportive place where caregivers can become educated and empowered to navigate through their challenging course.

That was the woman Tricia knew about when she asked if it was okay with me for her to fly to South Carolina and visit with my mom, who now lived every day vacant and silent. To me, it was as if all the things Mom had not found time to think about until now were surrounding her energy field, keeping most people at a distance. But Tricia is not most people. How many of your friends would fly on their own time and their own dime to visit your mother they had never met, much less your mother diminished by dementia? I told Tricia, honestly and from my heart, that I thought it was lovely that she wanted to see Mom. I really did not think she would. There are so many lessons in this one action. My friend Tricia listened to her instinct, she took action, and she let that be enough.

Doing the thing that makes you uncomfortable usually offers the greatest chance at growth. I love Eleanor Roosevelt's advice to do one thing every day that scares you. Did it scare Tricia to take the action to see my Mom? She had spoken on the phone with my father and had received his blessing for the visit as well, but I have to believe that when she walked into the Lowman Home, the skilled nursing facility where mom lived, and walked down the hall to my mother's room, she must have felt uncomfortable. Or maybe she did not.

I believe we rarely regret the things we do in life, only those things we fail to do. Tricia wanted to meet my mother while she was alive. She called me from the nursing home to describe the scene, mom's mood, what she was wearing. I felt comforted by the notion that mom would sense that love had entered the room. I saw an episode of Oprah with a brain surgeon who had a stroke. It was an ironic fate that gave her intimate knowledge during her years of recovery, which changed the way she lived her life and the way she treated her patients. It allowed her the kind of knowing that can only come from experiencing something. The doctor said even though she could not communicate with everyone who gathered around her after the stoke, she knew their intention and she felt their energy. She wrote a book about it and said that we all must be accountable for what we bring to any situation. I knew that Tricia would bring soothing energy of love to mom. I thought about how many chances I may have had to do that for others in my life and had left it undone, distracted by the feeling of being uncomfortable.

What Tricia did next was really beautiful. It was a bold, physical move that many of you reading this right now may have never done with your own mothers as an adult. She climbed into bed and curled up next to my mother. It was an intimate gesture that demonstrated Tricia's commitment to her own personal growth and to her quest to discover the truth about our capacity for human kindness.

At the Governor and First Lady's conference on women in Long Beach this year, my friend and mentor, Maria Shriver, spoke of a moment that had scared her. I smiled as I sat in the audience and heard her describe the scene. It was when she got into bed with her mother, Eunice Shriver, and risked the awkwardness, the loss of control, and the fear of intimacy that comes when our mothers are no longer the towers of physical and emotional strength is the moment when we recognize the wounded little girls inside of us that we want them to always be.

I learned a lot from Tricia's act of love. She showed that love is an action. Tricia made it a verb. I also discovered that pushing past the judgments that others place on us, or that we put upon ourselves, creates the perfect condition for growth. Intimate moments shared between people require that both sides are dedicated to allowing the exchange to be perfect, no matter how it unfolds. Life is most profound when we can give up the need to know what happens, the need to have an answer, or even to form the perfect questions.

"Life is most profound when we can give up the need to know what happens, the need to have an answer, or even to form the perfect questions."

- Leeza Gibbons

"She was forgetting, but she did not want to be forgotten."

- Leeza Gibbons

# *Words and Actions from Barbara*

"If there's anything I can do to help, just let me know." How often have we heard these words uttered in times of pain, loss, or crisis, and similarly, recall how we find ourselves offering this verbal kneejerk reaction to someone's difficult situation? For those of us who would truly like to help heal or support a family member, a colleague or even an acquaintance, I suggest asking yourself to go beyond merely saying the words and instead acting on them. How wonderful a world it would be if all the lovely intentions were translated into deeds of action and change.

The Dignity of Jeepers is an example of a grand act of love and friendship which was fulfilled.

If you can physically be with the person, go be with them. Clearly and directly ask them, "What can I do right now, at this very moment, that would be of the greatest help." If they have no answers find your own.

- *Fix something around the house*

- *Run an errand; make a stop at the cleaners, or the post office for your friend, does she have library books or DVD's that need to be returned? Take them back.*

- *Pick up a few extra items for your friend, when you are buying your own groceries.*

- *Help her children with their homework if you can, make sure they do their chores.*

- *Providing a sense of normalcy can be very comforting in difficult times.*

- *Find ways to entertain her children, it will brighten her day.*

# For You, I Wish

## Your Eternal Mother

*The rhythm of her heart soothed you long before you took your first breath of air. Her arms cradled you, her kisses smothered you. She held your hand, tied your shoes, brushed your hair. When you were scared, she reassured you, when you were sad, she comforted you. She knew you better than you knew yourself. She is your mother. Tonight you are asked to say goodbye to her, a quest too grand to comprehend. We are never ready to say goodbye to our mothers, regardless of age, for we are all the child looking up into her eyes when it is time to depart. She cannot hold you now. She cannot nurture your bleeding heart nor wipe the tears from your swollen eyes. Mother Nature knew we would all have to say goodbye to our mothers one day and that this departure would redefine our being and leave us hollow inside, so she gifted all of her children with maternal love; maternal love to share with one another when a mother must go. Your mother has wrapped her arms around many others in times of grief and heartache; now let them wrap their arms around you. Find your mother's love in all who love you. See her eyes twinkle through a baby's smile, feel her wisdom in a friend's devotion. In a field of daisies, rest your voice and look to the sky, remember the smell of her skin, the softness in her touch. The way her kiss took away the pain of a scrapped knee, the way her voice centered your world. As you feel her so close to you, let the rhythm of her heart soothe you once more and you will come to realize that you started off as one and became two. Now you are one again, this time it is she who lies within you, for she will forever be in your heart.*

"Mother Nature knew we would all have to say

goodbye to our mothers one day...

...so she gifted all of her children with maternal love..."

- Tricia LaVoice

# Reflection

*I was thinking of this Wish the other night while watching the 22-year-old Canadian ice skater accept her bronze metal only days after the sudden death of her mother. The audience thundered with applause as families across the world tuned in. It was hard to imagine what she could possibly be feeling. Tears streaming down my face, hurting for this young girl, I wondered if there is an age when it becomes easier to lose our mothers. I was thirty-one when my mother died and not even close to being done needing her love and guidance. I thought of all my friends who have lost their mothers, their ages, and if any of them had an easier time with their loss.*

*Vastly unfair, Leeza in the mid years of her life had to experience the loss of her mother twice. First, when the dreadful disease of Alzheimer's silenced her mother to her own world, and then again, when her body shut down. Barbara is in her mid fifties; her mother is 84. I think about when Barbara will have to say goodbye to her mother, and know it will be just as painful and difficult for her as it was for me.*

*After my mother died, I do not know if I was even conscious of it, but I managed to seek out maternal figures over the next decade to help fill that vast, dark hole of sadness. I have many friends my age, but over the years I befriended a handful of women, all about ten to twenty years older than me, and one more maternal than the next. They check in on me when I am not well, follow my children's achievements, and make sure I am being good to Rich. They are kind and gentle women, and the simple words of endearment they use when talking to me – Honey, Sweetie, Sweetheart – warm my heart all day long. When you do not have maternal love, you are so appreciative to receive it.*

*My one friend, Terese, bears a striking resemblance to my mother. I found her soon after my mother died, and then Barbara years later. They stepped into my life with such love and devotion that it prompted me to write a novel, Pieces of My Mother, which sits on my desk. In the book, I question whether my mother had sent these beautiful women to me, knowing how badly I was in need of maternal love. They were there at Grandparents Day events, birthdays, and holidays for my children. They make sure I am taking care of myself so I can better take care of my family. They make me feel like I belong.*

*When a mother is lost, we cannot replace her or stop the pain. However, we can reach inside of ourselves and love one another with the kindness of a maternal heart.*

" As a child my mother always told me, I am always with you,

right there on your shoulder, and I always will be.

I often find myself in moments of doubt, or concern,

whispering to my right shoulder."

– Barbara Lazaroff

# *Words and Actions from Barbara*

My mother Ellie, lost her mom at the age of four, and sadly, does not retain any memory of her except for stories others have related. Yet my mother, who did not have a caring relationship with her stepmother, miraculously revealed a deep reservoir of love and abiding strength when raising me and my two brothers. She demonstrated enormous resiliency, patience, courage and humor in the most difficult of times, and we always felt safe and cherished at home. She was my greatest cheerleader, always on my team, whether I won or lost. She taught me the importance of always trying my best, never giving up, being a team player when appropriate, and yet gave me the confidence to shine on my own with my best efforts and consistent dedication to a goal. I am blessed to still have her in my life. Although I cannot completely understand the loss, I try to be very supportive when a friend has to say goodbye to her mother. I cared for my dear girlfriend in the hospital and at home, and back to the hospital once again before she passed away. The complexity of feelings: tragic, enduring love, denial and disbelief, and finally acceptance permeated the room for weeks and weeks. Three generations stood guard. My dying friend protectively watched her identical twin daughters and her mother; her mother watched her extraordinary daughter suffer and ebb away, tenderly trying to shelter her granddaughters. My goddaughters were bereft in the knowledge that their mom was leaving them and yet, they held strong for their mother and grandmother. The tribe of friends held vigil, she was never alone. I slept in the hospital room and then one day at 4:06 p.m. she left us, and we cried and cried and cried, and held each other close. Another mother had left her children far too soon. Some thoughts on providing solace:

- *Lie on the bed with her or sit next to her on the couch, and let her weep. Do not try to contain the grief. Listen to her reminisce, hear her pain.*

- *If she needs and wants physical contact hold her hands, embrace her.*

- *Find a picture of her with her mother and put it in a locket.*

- *Call your friend on the first Mother's Day, her mother's birthday and the anniversary of her mother's passing.*

- Mail a weekly greeting card. If you knew her mother well, relate a memory.

- Send a box filled with her favorite treat, a fruit arrangement or nuts, (something healthy to fortify her), an uplifting DVD to watch, or a CD with calming music. Aromatherapy is a spirit lifter, or relaxer as well, essential oils with lovely scents, or a basket with lotions and bath salts.

- If you live nearby, go sit with her and read to her. Pick an uplifting book, something light, and each night read her a chapter or two.

- Wish for her every day. Start your morning by sending her a simple "Wish of the Day." It does not have to be poetic, just thoughtful.

- When we lose someone we love we do not want them to be forgotten. When she is ready to talk about memories and moments which she shared with her mother, be there for her and reinforce her healing process.

- If over time your friend becomes overly reclusive, or increasingly less verbal with friends and family, or starts having sleep, eating or work issues, it might be necessary to suggest a bereavement group or private counseling; help them follow through by either driving them there, attending with them or attempt an intervention.

"A woman is like a tea bag, you can't tell how strong she is
until you put her in hot water"
- Eleanor Roosevelt, Former First Lady

# A Tribute to
# Robert Graham

# For You, I Wish
## A Bow Good Night

*"Sculpt me a woman," you challenged my boy. I walked today through the winter's trees thinking of you, unsure of how a mother shows her respect to a man who has touched the soul of her child. I walked today through the winter's trees crying about you, not sure how a mother tells her son his mentor has passed. The trees surrounding me were bare of their leaves, their branches were brittle, and their bark had darkened in the frigid air. Yet, in the winter of my sadness, I see what I could not see before. A bird's nest perched high above the ground, once hidden in foliage, now clear to my eyes, a haven a mother so carefully sculpted to nurture her young. Her nest rests now, its work complete; but the life it held, the life it touched, is off soaring the skies before it too, will pause and sculpt a haven for its young. "Sculpt me a woman," you challenged my boy, the man with the hands gifted from heaven who now is soaring the skies. Your work is done, yet you live on in the hands and hearts of my child and in the hands and heart of all you have nurtured and touched. For you, Robert Graham, I bow and wish you good night.*

"Her nest rests now, its work complete,

but the life it held is off soaring the skies."

- Tricia LaVoice

# Reflection

*I met Robert Graham, the great sculptor, at an art showing Barbara brought me to shortly before my family moved from L.A. to Connecticut. I was aware that Robert Graham's work could be found in many prominent places across America, from the Roosevelt Memorial in D.C. to the Olympic Gateways in Los Angeles. However, witnessing his work firsthand was breathtaking.*

*As we left the show, Barbara introduced me to Robert Graham, and told him I had a son, Jack, who had shown a talent for sculpting. I asked him if he had any advice for me and he replied, "Tell him to give it away."*

*So we did just that. I spent a fortune at the art store buying clay, and Jack sculpted every chance he had and then gave his creations away as gifts. Two years later, I wrote Robert Graham a letter. I told him I was a mom from Connecticut with a ten-year-old son interested in art. I never mentioned that I had met him earlier or that I was friendly with people in Los Angeles that he may know. I simply asked if I could bring my son by his studio while visiting LA. His wonderful assistant replied promptly with a good time to stop by the studio.*

*Weeks later, I sat still while Jack was given a firsthand tour of the studio. As we went to leave, Jack handed Robert a piece of art he had made for him out of clay. Robert held it in his hands, looking down at Jack with so much emotion in his eyes. Then he excused himself for a moment and returned with one of his bronze pieces to give to Jack. This was the beginning of their sweet protégé/mentor relationship, the beginning of their respect for one another as artists.*

*Over the next two years, Jack flew to Los Angeles a couple of times to attend Robert's art showings and to visit him at his studio. During one of those visits, Jack asked Robert what his favorite animal was so he could sculpt it for him. Without hesitation, Robert replied, "Woman." Jack was challenged, so I came up with an idea and headed to the video store to rent The Addams Family movie starring Angelica Huston, Robert's wife of over fifteen years. Jack carefully sculpted a little Morticia Addams and mailed her off to Robert with a note saying, "Here is your favorite woman."*

*What touched me the most about Robert Graham's role in Jack's life was how unconditionally he gave to Jack. When we visited the studio, I would sit to the side and listen as Jack asked endless questions and Robert so patiently answered them. He took Jack in under his wing, sharing so much of himself but never asking for anything in return. One holiday, Robert made his friends and family art pieces out of clay and sent one to Jack with a note thanking him.*

*When Robert unexpectedly passed, telling Jack was one of the hardest things I have ever had to do. He was devastated. We decided to take him out of school and flew him to Barbara in Los Angeles to attend Robert Graham's memorial so he could pay his respects to the man, the teacher, the mentor who touched his heart ever so deeply, where he will always remain.*

# *Words and Actions from Barbara*

When we respect someone's artistry, intelligence, character, athletic prowess and they in return allow us to see ourselves through their eyes, filled with confidence in our potential, we are changed forever for the better. The loss of someone, who has shaped our life providing us with inspiration, is a tremendous bereavement, particularly for a young person. Usually a loss of this magnitude occurs with someone who we have forged a long relationship with over years of shared experiences, such as a parent, an extended family member, or a longtime teacher or friend. The situation with Tricia's son, Jack and Robert Graham was an unusual one. I had suggested that young Jack meet a professional artist, a genius sculptor such as Robert because Jack's reason for being was so completely entwined with his clay creations. When Robert passed away his death was devastating for Jack who thought he would have many more years of mentoring, and an ongoing friendship with the master. Tricia was conflicted with whether to tell Jack right away, and how to relate the sad news. Robert Graham's funeral was refined and would have done justice to a saint. Jack and I attended together; it was proper closure for a man of such talent and vision and an important moment for Jack, his special time to say goodbye. He brought a white dove he had been sculpting to give to Angelica Huston, Robert's widow. Tricia, as a sensitive mother, flew Jack across the country knowing this was essential for her son.

We also see how sometimes the length of time alone does not reflect the measure of impact someone can have on another's life. It reminds us that every interaction we have with another human being can be very powerful in both a positive or negative way. We must be mindful, especially with children, when we share our time with them. We can all be powerful influences in the life of a child, and we need to be accountable and conscientious with our words and actions.

- *Never underestimate your influence on a child's life, be a mentor.*

- *Indulge the child protégé passions and interests; if he loves to paint or sculpt take him to museums, art galleries, and art openings where he could meet the artist.*

- *If the child loves music, then escort her to a variety of different concerts. If you search you will find free ones in your community. If you can afford music lessons for the child, encourage her, listen to her practice, and applaud her progress, (even if initially the listening is difficult on the ears).*

- *If it is in your budget, dance lessons for the dancer, writing classes for the budding journalist, or buy them a journal, encourage him to write every day, offer to read the work unless he prefers to keep his work private. The internet and libraries offer many books on creative writing techniques.*

- *Encourage the young scientist by taking her to the planetarium, the local aquarium or seaside; perhaps there is a local lecture the two of you can attend by a guest speaker in her area of interest. If she is fascinated by the ocean and interested in marine biology, going snorkeling is great fun, and scuba diving is a great sport to learn.*

- *Communicate to him or her that you are proud of their effort and believe in their abilities. A good mentor is encouraging and thought provoking.*

- *Include them in activities with your family.*

- *Always be open to discussing the loss of a child's mentor, even if it is a painful process for you. If the mentor was your mom or dad, your child's fond memories will help heal you both.*

One of the most gratifying aspects of my life is the relationship I have forged with my various goddaughters. One of them, I had met at age five: I helped support her at certain moments through a difficult childhood, and her educational years. She honored me by asking if I would be the matron of honor at her wedding. She has now earned her PhD, and recently became a mother. All of my goddaughters have their own distinct personalities, intelligence and charm; they have all enriched my live.

This quote resonates with me more deeply,
the longer I am on this earth.

"We make a living by what we get,

we make a life by what we give."

- Sir Winston Churchill,
former Prime Minister of England

# For You, I Wish

## Honor

*I sat off to the side waiting, a woman next to me fumbled through her bag. The sounds of a father trying to calm his child competed with the typical hustle and bustle hums of the airport on a Tuesday afternoon. My eye caught notice of three women hurrying from window to window, anxiously awaiting the arrival of an aircraft. Obviously sisters, they giggled and pointed as the welcoming signs they made pressed against the window. Repeatedly, they asked one another, "Do you see her, do you see her?" Their excitement was enduring. I wondered curiously, was it a fourth sister they awaited? Their mother? But it became apparent that one of the women had more at stake than the other two. She bit her nails, wrapped her arms around her stomach, and paced at a feverish rate, her daughter, maybe returning from college, maybe on the eve of her wedding? As their plane arrived, I noticed I was not the only one in the waiting area giving them an audience, many of us watched with anticipation. One by one, men and women, boys and girls deplaned. Finally, a flight attendant reached the area and assured them, "She is on her way." The mother's expression mystified me, tears swelling in her eyes as she cupped her face with her shaking hands, but then it became clear. Her daughter appeared. She was beautiful, a child in her late teens, maybe early twenties, with long strawberry blonde hair and a face covered in freckles. Her uniform, shades of green and brown that are only worn by the U.S. Military. She dropped her gear as she reached out and buried her face in the chest of her mother. The waiting area burst in applause. The older gentlemen went first, but immediately, one by one, the waiting room stood. Tears flowed down many faces as this brave young solider desperately tried to stay strong. Someone yelled, "It's okay, soldiers cry too," and her body shook with emotion. A feeling of oneness, of unity, swept through the room as we all paid tribute to the example of courage and sacrifice before us. The applause held steady as they released their embrace but what happened next I will remember for the rest of my life. The young woman who risked her life for us and whose mind now holds unfathomable memories walked straight through the crowd. She never once stopped and asked anything of me or anyone else, she asked for nothing in return. I wish for you, the depth of this soldier's, and all those in service, honor.*

"I was envious of her passion for a cause;

a love of her country, that she would risk injury,

even her life, to be a soldier."

– Tricia LaVoice

# Reflection

*No matter how many times I read this Wish, tears come to my eyes when thinking about that day. I imagine not a moment goes by when a mother is not thinking about her child off at service. I think about how many times a day, or even week, I stop and think about our young soldiers, the sacrifice they are making for my country, my family, and my children, and I certainly know it is not nearly enough. Rarely do I think about the sacrifice their mothers and fathers are making, but this day shed light into the personal lives of military family life.*

*What this brave soldier taught me as she walked by us, her head held high, her eyes wet with tears, was the meaning of honor. I, for one, have never held such honor in my heart. In an odd way I was almost envious of her passion for a cause, a love of her country, that she would risk injury, even her life, to be a soldier. And more beautiful than her willingness to fight for her cause was her willingness to do so without asking for anything in return from those of us she is defending. Yes, the government pays them for their service but no one risks their lives, leaves their families, and lives in stressful conditions just for a paycheck. Honor, not money, gives them the strength to see it through another night.*

*It was wonderful to feel the vibration of applause run through the airport for this soldier, to watch the entire sitting area became one in emotion as we witnessed the raw display of love shared between this mother and daughter as they held on to one another in pure relief and gratitude. But the sacrifice is not just hers; her mother held on to her letting out sounds of joy that you knew came from the depth of her relief. To both the soldier and her mother, to all of our soldiers and all of their families, I would like to say, thank you.*

"These men and women courageously defend our freedom.
They are all someone's beloved child; they leave their
families to protect ours. Honor them, thank them,
remember them, always."

– Barbara Lazaroff

# *Words and Actions from Barbara*

Families with loved ones in the service experience stressful separation, fears and moments of loneliness. Upon their return many soldiers experience difficult re-entry into society. Some are physically or emotionally disabled and their lives are greatly altered. Some individuals can be rehabilitated, and others that have served our country with honor find that their marriages dissolve and there are no work opportunities. We should honor our soldiers abroad and at home and remember their service safeguards our freedom. There are countless ways we can show our respect and gratitude to those in the armed services, not only by supporting our military personnel but by supporting their families as well.

- *When you see a soldier out in public, bring your hand to your heart and look him or her in the eye as you nod your head, or if you are not this demonstrative, simply smile.*

- *If it is obvious he or she is with family, say thank you to all of them. This may feel awkward, but remember, that a soldier risks his or her life for your life. His or her family makes many sacrifices for your family's safety.*

- *If you are in a line at the store, bank or movies and see a soldier in uniform, ask them to please go first, express your feelings, tell them it would be your honor.*

- *Make cookies, drawings or write letters with your children, neighborhood children or a local school and bring them to a VA nursing home. Or send them abroad to our troops.*

- *You can "adopt" a particular veteran or share your time and resources with a few, by purchasing or loaning books, music CDs, or writing letters, delivering home cooked meals every week or once a month. Get a group of friends together, create an "Adopt a Veteran" club and rotate visiting days, talents and resources; by asking your friends to join you in this gesture of concern and appreciation for our soldiers, you rally the spirit of the entire community. Bring people who can teach the vets new skills and stimulating hobbies: photography, painting, computer programming, creative writing, music - maybe a guitar teacher. And for fun try darts, scrabble, or monopoly. Perhaps there is a person in your group who can entertain, play violin or piano, sing, or is genuinely funny. You need to know if the vets are welcoming of your involvement in their lives, some may be too private, or need solitude.*

- *Invite a soldiers' family over for a barbecue or dinner, or a weekend of relaxation, if you have a pool or garden, swim or plant flowers it is a nurturing activity, ask them to make themselves at home and read or just look at the sky and trees. You can watch a movie together, if you have a table play ping pong, try chess, checkers or cards. Entertain the soldier's children with creative projects at home, or take them to a zoo or park, or the planetarium.*

- *If the dad is the soldier and in the field, perhaps your son, husband or brother can play ball with their son. If the mother is the soldier and absent, the children may need some maternal love and support, and physical affection; take the girl for a manicure or hairstyling. Perhaps the boy needs a haircut, a new cool tee shirt, or just a friendly, fun trip to an ice cream parlor, to sit, talk and relax.*

- *Perhaps the children need a "stand in" mom or dad for an event at school.*

- *Just listening to the family, the spouse, the children, or the soldier's parents is very comforting for the soldier's family members.*

"How important it is for us to recognize and
celebrate our heroes and she—roes!"
- Maya Angelou, Poet and Author

# Wishes to Share

# For You, I Wish
## My Love and Gratitude

*Life holds precious gifts for us, unfolding them as we call on them. All are treasures, yet there is one immeasurable in value to the heart. This gift is living within the essence of all women, regardless of age, or if she has given birth or not; the gift to nurture, to value, to bestow maternal love. I ask, but what is a mother? She is the one who lifts you when your heart is dragging, the one who finds you when you have lost you, the one who stands silent so you can sing. She cares for you in illness, celebrates you in triumph, and encourages you in hardship. You are my friend; when I am down, you lift me up, when I am lost, you find me, and when I achieve, you celebrate me. I wish for you my love and gratitude.*

# For You, I Wish
## Your Eternal Mother

*The rhythm of her heart soothed you long before you took your first breath of air. Her arms cradled you, her kisses smothered you. She held your hand, tied your shoes, brushed your hair. When you were scared, she reassured you, when you were sad, she comforted you. She knew you better than you knew yourself. She is your mother. Tonight you are asked to say goodbye to her, a quest too grand to comprehend. We are never ready to say goodbye to our mothers, regardless of age, for we are all the child looking up into her eyes when it is time to depart. She cannot hold you now. She cannot nurture your bleeding heart nor wipe the tears from your swollen eyes. Mother Nature knew we would all have to say goodbye to our mothers one day and that this departure would redefine our being and leave us hollow inside, so she gifted all of her children with maternal love; maternal love to share with one another when a mother must go. Your mother has wrapped her arms around many others in times of grief and heartache; now let them wrap their arms around you. Find your mother's love in all who love you. See her eyes twinkle through a baby's smile, feel her wisdom in a friend's devotion. In a field of daisies, rest your voice and look to the sky, remember the smell of her skin, the softness in her touch. The way her kiss took away the pain of a scrapped knee, the way her voice centered your world. As you feel her so close to you, let the rhythm of her heart soothe you once more and you will come to realize that you started off as one and became two. Now you are one again, this time it is she who lies within you, for she will forever be in your heart.*

# For You, I Wish
## A River's Love

*All an entire river knows is to journey home, letting nothing stand in her way. In times of drought, she flows with calmness, low to the ground, not rousing the earth. In times of surge, she roars, rapidly racing her course. Place an obstacle in her way and she will overcome it with her determination and spirit squeezing under, over, and around the largest of boulders, the smallest of debris. All she knows is to journey home. All I know is to love you, letting nothing stand in my way. In times of struggle, I will remain gentle, providing you clarity. In times of conflict, I will move swiftly, softening your ache. If you detach from me, I will tenderly wait. If you place an obstacle in my way, I will trounce it, and if you find resentment and fury with me, I will humble myself. All the river knows is to journey home, as all I know is to love you. For you, I wish a river's love.*

# About

## Tricia LaVoice

Tricia LaVoice earned a Bachelor of Science degree in Applied Psychology from California State University, Long Beach and a Master's degree in Educational Psychology from Fordham University.

A stay at home mother of four, Tricia also enjoys writing for children and adults. Her first book, Helmets and Hoses, Toes and Noses, was released by Orchard Academy Press in July of 2008. Her second book, Pieces of My Mother is currently being reviewed for publication.

Leeza Gibbons has read many of Tricia's "Wishes" on her nationally syndicated radio program Hollywood Confidential. Tricia's writings can also be found on Leeza's website at www.LeezaGibbons.com.

Tricia lives in the countryside in Avon, Connecticut with her husband, daughter, three sons, and her dog and cats that accompany her on her long daily walks in nature. She is an avid yoga enthusiast and plants sunflowers everywhere she goes!

## Barbara Lazaroff

Restaurateur and interior designer Barbara Lazaroff, A.S.I.D. is renowned for her innovative restaurant concepts. As president of Imaginings Interior Designs, Inc., Barbara has designed such popular restaurants as the original Spago Hollywood, Spago Beverly Hills, Chinois in Santa Monica and Las Vegas, Eureka, Granita, and other noted dining establishments. She continues her work in the restaurant industry as a co-brander and partner in a multitude of "Wolfgang Puck" business entities and is a member of the Board of Directors of Wolfgang Puck Worldwide.

Barbara's unique concepts and designs have received critical acclaim and numerous awards. Her work has been featured in Designer's West, Restaurant Hospitality, Elle Décor, Fortune, Interiors, Restaurant/Hotel Design International, Luxe, and Vogue. She has been profiled on CNN, "Women on Top" a Canadian show about female entrepreneurs, Good Morning America, Home Show, Public Eye, Interior Motives, West 57th, among others. In 1991 Barbara was inducted into the prestigious Platinum Circle of design professionals by Restaurant/Hotel Design International. She received an honorary degree of Doctor of Business Administration in Hospitality Management from Johnson and Wales University in 1998. In 2000 Barbara was inducted into the National Association of Women Business Owners Millennium Hall of Fame, which noted her leadership and business acumen.

In 1982, Barbara co-founded, the annual American Wine and Food Festival, which funds the Puck-Lazaroff Charitable Foundation whose sole mission is providing key support for the Meals on Wheels Program in L.A.. In 1984, she co-founded the annual California Spirit event which supports the American Cancer Society. Barbara has hosted an annual Spago Passover Seder benefitting Mazon since 1984, providing hunger relief in the community. Most notable among her many charitable honors are the James Beard Humanitarian Award, and the Aviva Family and Children's Services' Spirit of Compassion Award, an organization close to her heart. Barbara recently completed a four year remodel of one of the Aviva residences. Barbara serves on the Board of Directors of The Friends of Sheba Medical Center, located in Israel.

In addition, Barbara is engaged in a number of organizations that promote women in the hospitality industry, and the political and design arenas. She is one of the founding members of Women Chefs and Restaurateurs. Barbara is launching a weekly show for Jewish Life Television (JLTV), as well as a line of home furnishings and accessories. She is passionate collector, and a patron of the arts. Barbara resides in Beverly Hills, with her two sons, her longtime beau, and a menagerie of pets.

www.barbaralazaroff.com
www.awff.org   American Wine and Food Festival
www.calspirit.org   California Spirit Event
www.avivacenter.org   Aviva Family and Children's Services

## Leeza Gibbons

She has been called a social entrepreneur, but if you ask Leeza Gibbons what she does, she'll simply answer "I'm a storyteller". From television news journalist and host, to radio personality, producer and businesswoman, Leeza has been entering America's living rooms for over 25 years. While she would nationally burst on the scene as an anchor & reporter on ENTERTAINMENT TONIGHT, it wouldn't be until hosting her own daytime talker LEEZA that audiences would see Gibbons' determination to get outside of the box and become a household name while highlighting her intelligence, sensitivity and compassion. Gibbons served as Executive Producer of LEEZA, which debuted on NBC in 1994 and continued nationally through 2000. Receiving nominations for both Outstanding Talk Show and Outstanding Talk Show Host every year it was eligible, LEEZA would garner 27 Daytime Emmy Nominations, winning three. It was during the series run that Gibbons' impact on television would be awarded with one of Hollywood's highest honors: a star on the Hollywood Walk of Fame. With her never-ending entrepreneurial creativity and a mind for business-building, Gibbons formed LEEZA GIBBONS ENTERPRISES (LGE) in 1994, and since then she has produced and developed the kinds of projects, partnerships and products that reflect her passions and concerns.

Leeza Gibbons hosts and produces the nationally syndicated radio program HOLLYWOOD CONFIDENTIAL which is featured on over 125 radio stations across the country and internationally and is now entering its 16th year in production.

With SHEER INSPIRATION LIFE COACHING, Leeza demonstrates her ongoing efforts to find creative ways to reach her audience and offer life-changing support. Sheer Inspiration is an innovative web business which supplies users with a personal coach via email and/or phone to tackle a variety of challenges ranging from parenting and health to relationships.

She lives with her three children in Los Angeles.

To learn more about Leeza's foundation visit www.leezasplace.org

A special thank you to Jan Miller, Shannon Marven, sweet
Lacy Lynch and the team of Dupree /Miller and Associates
for their continuous support and tireless effort.

# Wishes Inc.
1158 26th Street, #680
Santa Monica, CA 90403

## Patricia LaVoice
tricia@wishesfortheheart.com

## Barbara Lazaroff
barbara@wishesfortheheart.com